24 0808403 3

TELEPEN

WITHDRA

D0120365

Euronotes and Euro-commercial paper

Gareth Bullock, BA

Executive Director of Swiss Bank
Corporation International Limited

London
Butterworths
1987

341.41 B

United Kingdom	Butterworth & Co (Publishers) Ltd, 88 Kingsway, LONDON WC2B 6AB and 61A North Castle Street, EDINBURGH EH2 3LJ
Australia	Butterworths Pty Ltd, SYDNEY, MELBOURNE, BRISBANE, ADELAIDE, PERTH, CANBERRA and HOBART
Canada	Butterworths. A division of Reed Inc., TORONTO and VANCOUVER
New Zealand	Butterworths of New Zealand Ltd, WELLINGTON and AUCKLAND
Singapore	Butterworth & Co (Asia) Pte Ltd, SINGAPORE
South Africa	Butterworth Publishers (Pty) Ltd, DURBAN and PRETORIA
USA	Butterworth Legal Publishers, ST PAUL, Minnesota, SEATTLE, Washington, BOSTON, Massachusetts, AUSTIN, Texas and D & S Publishers, CLEARWATER, Florida

© Gareth Bullock 1987

All rights reserved. No part of this publication may be reproduced or transmitted in any form or by any means, including photocopying and recording, without the written permission of the copyright holder, application for which should be addressed to the publisher. Such written permission must also be obtained before any part of this publication is stored in a retrieval system of any nature.

This book is sold subject to the Standard Conditions of Sale of Net Books and may not be re-sold in the UK below the net price fixed by Butterworths for the book in our current catalogue.

British Library of Cataloguing in Publication Data

Bullock, Gareth
    Euronotes and euro-commercial paper.
    1. International finance   2. Euro-dollar
    market   3. Euro-bond market
    I. Title
    332.4'54   HG3881
ISBN 0 406 10410 7 ✓

BULLOCK

29 JUN 1987

ACCESSION
NUMBER 808403

CLASS
NUMBER

Typeset by Phoenix Photosetting, Chatham, Kent
Printed and bound in Great Britain by
Mackays of Chatham Ltd, Kent

Preface

Rarely has the banking business seen such intense activity as that caused by the advent of the euronote and its subsequent development into the Euro-commercial paper market. It has been for all those involved in the market a quite extraordinary experience. More than one borrower has expressed complete bewilderment at the array of terms, acronyms and claims heard from the large number of commercial and investment banks pressing upon it a 'NIF' or 'RUF'. One of the aims of this book is to dispel that confusion.

This book aims to provide a history, description and analysis of the euronote as an instrument and of the market in which it is actively bought and sold. In order to achieve this I have chosen to follow the chronology of the market's development – from the attempts of the early 1970s to the present day's Euro-commercial paper market. Within that chronology I have sought to identify the key trends which have been most influential in furthering the evolutionary process. Whilst that entails description it also calls for detailed analysis of the changing environment for banks, investors and borrowers as well as the distribution techniques established by various market participants.

The book aims also to provide a comprehensive analysis of the technical and legal aspects of euronotes and Euro-commercial paper. It must be said (without underestimating the task of the euronote salesman or trader) that the technical side of euronotes as a money-market instrument is relatively straightforward. Basic calculations and conventions are described whereas the complex intricacies of the trading and funding of euronotes and Euro-commercial paper are left to specialist publications on money-market instruments as a generic subject.

Some degree of subjectivity has been necessary and where this is the case I have sought a consensus view through consulting with other colleagues actively involved in this market. Where strong difference of opinion exists, this is significant of itself and both views are consequently represented in the text.

I am extremely grateful to the many contributors whose assistance has brought the task of writing this book to fruition. A major contribution to the complete understanding of the confusing subject of settlement has been made by Alan Taylor, formerly of the First Chicago Clearing Centre, in his preparation of Chapter 6. Similarly, I hope that Chapter 7 on 'Legal Aspects' may become used as the comprehensive guide to the all-important US legal implications on euronotes and Euro-commercial paper. My thanks to Greer L Phillips, Edmond Robinson and Manley O Hudson Jr of Cleary, Gottlieb, Steen and Hamilton for their professional efforts. I am also grateful to Steven Edelman, partner at Linklaters and Paines, for his contribution on English law in that chapter. I am most indebted to Paul Goldschmidt, formerly of Goldman Sachs International Corporation, for his insight into the early attempts at Euro-commercial paper and indeed, to William M Valiant, Vice President and Treasurer of Borg-Warner Corporation for providing valuable information and materials about those early attempts. John Hughes, Senior Vice President and Jim Jack, Executive Vice President of Associates Corporation of North America were very helpful in providing information and material on Associates' own early programme. For much of the statistical information I am grateful to both International Financing Review (IFR) and Euromoney whose excellent record-keeping has become so important to participants in this market. It is kind of Britoil plc, the Swedish National Debt Office and Export Development Corporation of Canada to permit publication of details of their issuance of euronotes and Euro-commercial paper. Goldman Sachs Money Markets Inc are to be thanked for providing some of the charts and tables which are of their usual high standard. Additionally, I am grateful for the comments, advice and assistance of Nicholas F-R Dungan, Brian Woolley, Andrew Reicher, Morven Jones, Gillian Nicholas, Rosemary Carawan, Rupert Dent and Martin Short. Last, but not least, grateful thanks to Shirley Crane for bringing order out of chaos in the manuscript.

Gareth Bullock

Contents

Abbreviations

BONUS	Borrower's option for notes and underwritten standby
CD	certificate of deposit
CTP	continuous tender panel
EDC	Export Development Corporation of Canada
FCCC	First Chicago Clearing Centre
GCM	General Council's Memorandum
ISM	issuer set margin
LIBID	London Interbank Bid Rate
LIBOR	London Interbank Offered Rate
OFDI	Office of Foreign Direct Investments
RUF	revolving underwriting facility
SEC	Securities and Exchange Commission
SOY	strike offering yield
TEFRA	Tax Equity and Fiscal Responsibility Act 1982

CHAPTER 1

Early attempts

We have to look back to the early 1970s to find the first public attempts to establish a Euro-commercial paper market. From today's vantage-point the early 1970s seem halcyon days for commercial banks. Foreign banks, of which most had had offices in London for some decades, were in expansionist mood. US banks, in particular, had built up significant operations aiming to service the large number of domestic US corporate customers which had expanded into the European market during the 1950s and 1960s. As London became the centre of the Eurodollar market the number of banks represented there by a branch, subsidiary or representative office increased from 138 in 1969 to 263 by 1975. Competition was strong but in a growing market. Lending Eurodollars to corporate and sovereign borrowers was considered prime business for commercial banks, especially at a time when lending margins on short-term funds were typically ½% or more and on medium-term loans margins of 1% or more were certainly not uncommon. On the face of it, therefore, it did not seem that there were any fundamental reasons why a Euro-commercial paper market should appear in this environment. Risk diversification by investors was generally achieved by adding more banks to their approved deposits list rather than seeking non-bank investment instruments. In the absence of these fundamentals it required some external, artificial stimulus for a Euro-commercial paper market to develop. This came in the form of specific US legislation affecting how US companies could finance their overseas subsidiaries and affiliates.

The United States government in 1968 first established the Office of Foreign Direct Investments ('OFDI') and promulgated regulations which established certain restrictions on US business enterprises making transfers of capital abroad. Companies which had a 10% (or greater) investment in a foreign corporation were designated 'direct investors' and were subject to these restrictions. The permissible annual amount of direct investment was set at a percentage of the average positive direct investment made by the company during the base years 1965 and 1966. That percentage was related to the geographic area (called a 'schedule') receiving the investment but for Europe it was either 65% or 35% depending on the country. Certain provisions of the OFDI regulations permitted US companies (or their finance subsidiaries) to raise long-term foreign borrowings which could be used as an offset to direct investment. For example, if a US company made an investment of $1,000,000 in a foreign subsidiary and used the proceeds of a long-term foreign borrowing for this purpose, the transfer of capital amounted to $1,000,000 against which the company could make a deduction of the same amount, the effect being a zero net transfer of capital. A key definitional element of a long-term foreign borrowing was that it would not ordinarily be repaid within 12 months of the original date of its being made.

1

If, according to the base-year calculation, a US company had a permissible annual direct investment limit of $10,000,000, it could effect the investment by raising the amount from its domestic finance sources. If it required in total say, $25,000,000 for its overseas subsidiary, it would have to raise the additional $15,000,000 through local borrowings. If the local borrowing came under the definition of a long-term foreign borrowing then it could be offset, as described above, against the permissible direct investment. Since such foreign borrowings, in order to qualify for an offset, were necessarily of a long-term (over 12 months) and somewhat inflexible nature, some companies chose not to borrow in this way. These companies, as well as others for which long-term borrowings did not satisfy their total financing need, were obliged to use the short-term finance markets. In almost all cases this obliged companies to access the bank loan market which proved to be more expensive than the domestic short-term finance sources available to US companies, of which commercial paper was usually the most competitive.

The financial penalty imposed on companies by OFDI was severe. Their cheapest domestic alternative source of short-term funds was commercial paper and this enjoyed at times a cost advantage (including dealers' commissions) of as much as 100 basis points compared to the Euromarket pricing benchmark of the London Interbank Offered Rate ('LIBOR'). The cost penalty of having to finance offshore was compounded by the fact that the lending margin on any Eurodollar borrowing facility would generally have been higher than the commitment fees payable on back-up facilities required to support US commercial paper programmes. Therefore if the US commercial paper/LIBOR differential was 1%, the Eurodollar facility lending margin 0.50% pa and the domestic commitment fee 0.375% pa, the US borrower would be paying 1.125% pa more than if it had been able to finance itself domestically.

Against this background it seems only logical that US companies should have sought to replicate in the Euromarkets a commercial paper market based on the US model with which they were so familiar and comfortable. The impetus, not unnaturally, came mainly from the US investment banks which had been acting as dealers on domestic commercial paper programmes for several years. Not only were they familiar with the concept, structure and techniques of the commercial paper product but it was their *own* domestic customers who required a solution to a difficult problem. It is worth re-emphasising here that the problem relating to sources of finance came about purely because of the OFDI programme and therefore only concerned US companies.

In response to this problem a number of major US companies therefore established in late 1971 what were called 'Euro-commercial paper programmes'. The methodology of these programmes borrowed almost entirely from the domestic commercial paper market. A programme was uncommitted, ie no formal bank commitment was connected with the programme. The company was prepared to issue short-term promissory notes to investors willing to accept a given yield and maturity. A bank calling itself a 'dealer' would act as intermediary in order to place these notes with investors at the right yield and maturity. For this placement activity it would earn a commission. It is estimated that over a dozen major US companies entered the market, the first being such well known names as Woolworth International

Credit Corporation (guaranteed by FW Woolworth Company), Borg-Warner Corporation, Continental Can Company, Bristol-Myers Company and Goodyear Tyre & Rubber Company. Despite the prefix 'Euro', the prime mover amongst the banks in developing the new market was not a European bank but Goldman Sachs & Company, the US investment bank which had and continues to have a dominant position in the domestic commercial paper market.

The real benefit for US companies was to be able to classify Euro-commercial paper borrowings as 'long-term foreign borrowings' for OFDI purposes. The OFDI regulations had stipulated that borrowings of less than 12 months would not qualify as such. The regulations were amended to permit the qualification of borrowings which were not repaid within 12 months even if they were a continuous series of short-term borrowings (say, three or six months). Euro-commercial paper programmes would therefore qualify as a long-term foreign borrowing for OFDI purposes, provided the notes could be refinanced at each maturity for a period of at least 12 consecutive months. This, of course, was a material stimulus to the Euro-commercial paper market and enabled US companies to use a flexible borrowing method rather than the alternative of a long-term Eurobond issue.

The cost dynamics of deciding whether to establish a Euro-commercial paper programme were relatively simple. Faced with the alternative of borrowing directly from its banks at LIBOR plus ½% (or often higher) the borrower needed to issue notes under a Euro-commercial paper programme as well as negotiate a commitment fee on the back-up credit lines with its banks at a combined cost lower than this direct bank borrowing cost. The borrower was thus exposed to two risks: one, the investor market for its paper might not remain consistently competitive as to price and amount; and, two, that banks might not be willing to make commitments available at a reasonable cost.

We must not miss here an early example of a trend which will become crucial in the development of a lasting Euro-commercial paper market. Borrowers, hand in hand with their investment bank advisers, were participating, perhaps unwittingly, in the process of 'disintermediating' commercial banks. Disintermediation is a term which we shall come across later in this book and can be defined as the lending of funds by creditor to debtor without the usual intermediary function being provided by a bank's balance sheet. At its most simplistic, commercial banking entails the taking of deposits (thereby recording a liability on one side of the balance sheet) and the lending of those funds at a higher rate of interest (thereby recording an asset on the other side of the balance sheet). The interest differential accrues as income. Clearly, in a large and diversified commercial bank specific deposits are not on-lent as specific assets. However, in a Euro-commercial paper programme the process is creditor-and debtor-specific. By selling to an investor a bearer instrument which denotes a financial obligation of the issuer, a commercial bank balance sheet is not involved: issuer and investor are put into a direct contractual relationship with each other. If the issuer cannot repay the note, the investor loses its money. This can be contrasted with the investor depositing its money with a commercial bank which has already made a loan to a company which ultimately goes into bankruptcy – the investor or, rather, depositor will lose all or part of its money only if the bank collapses as a result of that bad loan. The simple reality is that through the bearer note the investor is directly exposed to the risk of a single issuer; it must be able to assess that risk adequately and be comfortable with it. The investor's attitude to the new instrument is an important aspect of the development of the Euro-commercial paper market and it is remarkable how many investors considered the purchase of a bearer note issued by a corporate or a sovereign borrower as an entirely different decision from making a time-deposit with a commercial bank, as though the latter action was risk-free. We shall see how this attitude crucially changed in later years and became a fundamental reason for the rise of the Euro-commercial paper market.

Another term which has now come into everyday bankers' jargon but nonetheless denotes a vital trend is 'securitisation'. It goes hand in hand with disintermediation and, indeed, it has become the catalyst for disintermediation. It describes the process whereby debt is changed into easily transferable and negotiable form through being issued as a security, normally a bearer instrument. Instead, therefore, of fixed advances being made by a bank to a borrower under a short-term loan agreement of several pages, the debt obligation is enshrined in a bearer security and is thus able to be sold from investor to investor with each new holder enjoying full creditor rights against the issuer of the security.

These early programmes tended to use a promissory note made out to the order of the dealer and endorsed by the latter without recourse – this had the effect of making Euro-commercial paper freely negotiable. A legend on the note prevented sales to US or Canadian investors. Notes were issued at a discount to face value and the denominations of the notes could be as little as $10,000 but on average sales were executed at the $1,000,000 level. Maturities tended to be limited to three and six months, the usual maturities at the time for Eurodollar certificates of deposit (short-term debt securities issued by banks).

As far as cost was concerned, Euro-commercial paper was typically offered at LIBOR plus 0.25% pa thus offering a yield to investors above that on Euro-CDs. On top of this the Euro-commercial paper dealer would add its commission. Unlike domestic commercial paper, Euro-commercial paper was traded in the secondary market though, whilst dealers claimed they would maintain a secondary market, it is not possible to gauge how successful or frequent such trading was.

At the time of these early programmes there was no established sophisticated investor base which could or would spend time analysing the credit risk of potential Euro-commercial paper issuers. The key to achieving investor acceptance of the issuers' risk was to bring to the market only those companies which were extremely well known and which had good official agency debt ratings (in practice, normally Moody's Investors Service and Standard & Poors). Indeed, the companies who did enter the market tended to be large multi-nationals which at the time typically had a long-term debt rating of AA by the major rating agencies. This rating meant that they were judged to be of high quality by all standards. They were also well known by the small banks and large insurance companies which formed the core of the investor base to which dealers aimed their note placement efforts. In denoting a strong financial condition the rating was a proxy for credit quality. Statistics are unreliable at the best of times in the Euro-commercial paper market, even

Example of Euro-commercial paper note from the early 1970s

No. _____ U.S. Dollars

LONDON, ENGLAND

_____ 19 _____

On _____ 19 _____ For Value Received we irrevocably and unconditionally promise

(Maturity Date) to pay to BEARER

The sum of _____ U.S. Dollars

At the London Office of _____

This note will be paid without deduction for any taxes imposed by the United States or any political subdivision thereof.

_____

Issuing Agent

By _____ By _____

Countersignature Authorized Signature

This Note shall not be validly issued until countersigned by Issuing Agent.

THIS DEBT OBLIGATION IS TO BE TREATED AS THE DEBT OBLIGATION OF A FOREIGN OBLIGOR FOR PURPOSES OF THE UNITED STATES INTEREST EQUALIZATION TAX AND ITS ACQUISITION BY A UNITED STATES PERSON SHALL SUBJECT SUCH PERSON TO TAX LIABILITY, WITHOUT REGARD TO ANY EXEMPTION OR EXCLUSION IN CHAPTER 41 OF THE INTERNAL REVENUE CODE, AT THE RATE OF TAX APPLICABLE UPON THE ACQUISITION OF OUTSTANDING STOCK.

today, but it is estimated that at the height of the market in 1973 about US$ 2 billion of notes were outstanding. Progamme size depended on the issuer's need, with some as little as $25 million and others as much as $200 million.

We saw above the simple economics of deciding to set up a Euro-commercial paper programme. Outstanding paper of US$ 2 billion suggests that for a number of companies those economics were beneficial compared to direct bank borrowings. Yet this may not have been true in all cases. Commercial banks operating in the Euromarkets, especially US banks, saw the potential dangers to them of the disintermediation process; it would mean the loss of their profitable short-term lending business. Indeed, the US banks were already losing their domestic US short-term corporate lending business through increasing substitution by domestic commercial paper. The Glass-Steagall Act prevented commercial banks from becoming commercial paper dealers which would have enabled them to recoup the foregone income on corporate lending. In the Euromarkets, however, commercial banks were not powerless to stop this process in what could be seen as a case of 'once bitten, twice shy'.

Their competitive response was twofold. First, they could and did lower the margins on their loans to those customers potentially capable of setting up a Euro-commercial paper programme. This course of action put pressure on the comparative economics of the Euro-commercial paper programme although it had its disadvantages in that it reduced the banks' return on assets and absolute earnings levels. Indeed, faced with the need to finance in the Euromarkets because of the OFDI regulations, a number of companies' first approach was to negotiate, with some success, lower local borrowing margins with their banks. Second and crucially, the banks were still needed in a Euro-commercial paper programme to provide back-up lines of credit, for if the market for the notes dried up, the issuer would need the safety-net of bank financing. The cost of this commitment was a vital element of the overall economics of a programme and some banks were insistent on commitment fee levels which rendered those economics unviable. With the potential disappearance of their short-term loan business many banks were sufficiently strongly motivated to risk customer relationships by not co-operating in charging commitment fees on back-up facilities at levels which made Euro-commercial paper issuance an economic alternative, One issuer whose programme at the time only managed $2 million outstandings for 90 days commented succinctly: 'the banks wouldn't play ball'.

Banks are rarely forthcoming about investors in various types of securities for fear of giving too many secrets away. Our knowledge of the investor base for the early programmes suffers as a result. With notes denominated as high as $1,000,000 it was always conceived as a 'professional' market. Principle investor groups were banks and large institutions such as insurance companies which were capable of analysing credit risk. Some banks saw it as an opportunity effectively to lend to companies of excellent credit standing with whom they previously had little or no contact. It was not necessary even to have visited the company to make a loan and in a market where most banks were looking to expand their corporate business relationships and to increase their loan portfolios there was no potential shortage of lenders. Institutional investors normally kept a proportion of their investible funds in short-term instruments such as certificates of deposit (CDs) or in time-deposits with banks. The yield on these investments was unlikely to be higher than the

London Interbank Bid Rate ('LIBID' – defined usually as ⅛% below LIBOR). A note, therefore, yielding above LIBID (and probably above LIBOR) represented an attractive investment especially if the issuer was well known and its long-term debt obligations formally rated AA or better.

It is appropriate at this point to describe briefly the operational mechanics of such Euro-commercial paper programmes. Modelled on the domestic commercial paper programmes they used a bank as a dealer to place with investors paper issued under the programme. Typically, when the issuer required funds it would discuss with its dealer (or dealers) the optimum maturity and interest rate level in the light of market conditions and then issue notes accordingly. The dealer would normally act as agent rather than principal, ie it would sell notes to investors on behalf of the issuer only when it had firm investor demand. In some circumstances when the issuer had an urgent need which exceeded immediate investor demand, the dealer might hold notes on its own books but would probably have quoted a higher yield to the issuer because of the risk involved. The notes were issued by an issuing agent who authenticated them by signature and transferred them to the order of the investor in exchange for payment to the issuer's bank account. In cases where paper for whatever reason could not be issued sufficient for the company's immediate needs the company would seek funds, most probably from its banks, until it could issue paper again.

In most cases notes issued under Euro-commercial paper programmes were discount notes, ie they did not bear a coupon but were issued at less than their face value to produce the desired yield. If a $1,000,000 note of 90 days' maturity were purchased by the investor at a discount to yield of 7½% the following calculation would be made to determine the consideration paid by the investor:

(a) Discount rate

$$\text{Consideration} = \frac{NV}{1 + \left(\dfrac{Y \times D}{36000}\right)}$$

Where: NV = the nominal (or face) value of the note
   Y = the purchase yield for the investor
   D = the remaining number of days to maturity

Therefore, $$\frac{1,000,000}{1 + \left(\dfrac{7.5 \times 90}{36000}\right)}$$

$$= \frac{1,000,000}{1.01875}$$

$$= US\$\,981,595.09$$

If, however, it had been an interest-bearing 90-day note which bore a coupon of 7% and the investor had purchased it at a yield of 7½%, the following calculation of the consideration payable by the investor would be made:

(b) Interest-bearing note

$$\text{Consideration} = \text{NV} \times \left(\frac{(C \times M) + 36000}{(Y \times D) + 36000}\right)$$

Where: NV = the nominal (or face) value of the note
C = the coupon on the note
M = the original number of days in the note's maturity
Y = the purchase yield of the investor
D = the remaining number of days till maturity

$$\text{Therefore,} \qquad 1{,}000{,}000 \times \left(\frac{(7 \times 90) + 36000}{(7.5 \times 90) + 36000}\right)$$

$$= 1{,}000{,}000 \times \left(\frac{36630}{36675}\right)$$

$$= 1{,}000{,}000 \times 0.99877301$$

$$= \text{US\$ } 998{,}773.01$$

It would have been most interesting to refine our knowledge of this nascent investor base and to track the processes of disintermediation and securitisation, had the market not abruptly stopped at the beginning of 1974. In February of that year the OFDI regulations were repealed and with their cessation US companies were then able to fund their overseas operations, as they had wanted to, by freely using their own domestic markets or whichever market was most cost-effective. The Euro-commercial paper market had been founded on 100% US company involvement and very quickly every company forsook the recently established market for other considerably cheaper sources of debt. The new market collapsed, proving once again that government regulations do not represent the real economic fundamentals required if a market is to provide lasting value to both buyer and seller.

Because the market vanished a number of questions remain tantalisingly unanswerable. What would have been the commercial banks' strategic response to Euro-commercial paper? How far would disintermediation have gone and would non-US companies have entered the market? How would the investor base have developed? Would a retail market have been possible? Would note pricing have remained tied to LIBOR? It would be some ten years before these questions could begin to be answered. Indeed, if any circumstances might have arisen immediately after the repeal of the OFDI regulations which would have resuscitated a Euro-commercial paper market, they were dashed by the removal of fiscal barriers in the US which had precluded non-US borrowers from entering the domestic money markets, most importantly, the commercial paper market. High quality non-US issuers, which would have been prime issuers in any Euro-commercial paper market, entered the domestic commercial paper market from July 1974 onwards. For US and non-US issuers alike the focus of competitively-priced short-term dollar funds fell continuously for the next ten years on the domestic commercial paper market. Outstandings of foreign issuers in the domestic commercial paper market rose steadily throughout the late 1970s and reached as much as $8.4 billion by the end of 1980. The total today has exceeded $40 billion.

These early Euro-commercial paper programmes applied only to US issuers and flowered in a hothouse created by a temporary regultory climate rather than by fundamental economic stimuli. It is hardly surprising that they should therefore have disintegrated once the regulatory climate changed. Their disappearance, however, did not kill off the concept of a Euro-commercial paper market and it continued to remain an obvious option for the Euromarkets. A real market could only be produced in a lasting environment brought about by fundamental economic reasons and it is the emergence of this environment that will be described and analysed in the forthcoming chapters.

CHAPTER 2

The euronote arrives

Short-term lending activities in the Euromarkets were largely confined from mid-1974 until 1980 to direct bank lending. The dramatic rise in oil prices in 1973, as is now known, gave rise to enormous, continuing liquidity in the banking system and much of the re-cycling of those so-called petro-dollars was effected through commercial bank lending. The mid-to-late 1970s saw as a consequence increasing competition amongst banks to lend Eurodollars to their customers and, with such an overwhelming supply of funds set against strong but not excessive demand, lending margins continuously declined. Indeed, they have declined steadily without respite to the present day. During this period the number of banks involved in Eurodollar lending rose dramatically. Loans syndicated by a lead manager amongst a group of banks became a typical financing structure, especially as the size of loan facilities required by borrowers became larger. If competition to participate was strong, competition to win the mandate from a borrower to lead manage such a facility became increasingly intense. It was in this competitive environment that an innovative borrowing structure was born, a structure which would be the first step along the road to a fully-fledged Euro-commercial paper market.

THE NOTE PURCHASE FACILITY

It was the then-called Citicorp International Bank Limited, the investment banking arm of Citibank NA, which created this borrowing structure in a US$ 30 million facility it arranged in December 1978 for the New Zealand Shipping Corporation. This borrower, which was guaranteed by Her Majesty in Right of New Zealand, represented a prime credit risk and was the subject of strong competition amongst a number of experienced banks seeking its mandate to arrange a financing. For the borrower the key factor, of course, was cost. For the banks it was to win the mandate without cutting lending margins even further and thereby setting a dangerous pricing precedent for future transactions. Looked at in plain commercial banking terms the choice was stark; there was little room for manœuvre other than to cut the lending margin or the commitment fee or both. The idea that won the mandate demonstrated a considerable degree of lateral thinking in that it looked at the problem not only in terms of traditional commercial banking but also in terms of the securities market.

The transaction recognised that there can be two basic elements to a credit facility. First, the essential credit insurance provided to a borrower by a bank, that is, when the borrower wants to borrow funds, the bank will be legally obliged to advance funds on pre-agreed terms. If a bank is prepared to lend money to a borrower for a period of years, it is logical that it should also be prepared to 'insure' or guarantee availability of funds in the event that the borrower avails itself temporarily of funds from another source. Indeed, if the provider of funds from another source is on risk for the tenor of its loan, then the 'insurer' can argue that its own risk vis-à-vis the borrower may even be somewhat less. Second, there is the element of drawn funds and the critical innovation of the New Zealand Shipping Corporation was the recognition that the drawn funds element need not be a direct advance by the same bank that provides the credit insurance. What this facility recognised in the securities market was the attraction to investors of Euro-certificates of deposit (Euro-CDs) which are short-term bearer instruments issued in US dollars by banks for maturities of usually one, three and six months. The Euro-CD market was at that time relatively mature and active; logic demanded that investors would be attracted by an instrument identical in nature except that it was issued by a high quality government-guaranteed entity rather than a bank. This raises the important question of why short-term debt instruments needed to be issued exclusively by banks when there was potentially available a wide range of non-bank issuers of equivalent or better risk.

The product of this thinking was christened a committed note purchase facility. As its size was relatively small at US$ 30m (and owing to Citicorp's probable desire to maintain the secrecy of the facility's exact structure and operation) Citicorp was the sole provider of credit insurance. Under the terms of the agreement the New Zealand Shipping Corporation could issue throughout the six-year tenor of the facility notes of either a three or six month maturity. Citicorp provided a commitment for the whole tenor of the facility to purchase these notes at a margin above LIBOR contractually agreed in the documentation. It thus gave the borrower a committed source of funds at a known price. If the borrower did not wish to draw down funds, it did not issue notes but paid a commitment fee instead just as in a traditional revolving credit facility. Citicorp could hold the notes if it wished but generally sought to sell the notes to investors whose normal investment practice hitherto was to buy Euro-CDs. It is understood that the notes were sold around $\frac{1}{8}$% pa above LIBOR, which was a significant yield improvement for investors accustomed to Euro-CD yields of LIBID at best. The yield at which Citicorp bought the notes from the New Zealand Shipping Corporation has not been made public but, logically, it would have been at a level which assured Citicorp a sales commission or 'turn' but which in absolute terms represented for the borrower a cost cheaper than that of a normal revolving credit facility in the commercial bank market at the time. For example, if the then prevailing market conditions suggested $\frac{3}{8}$% pa above LIBOR as the optimum cost of a revolving credit facility and the borrower's short-term notes could reasonably be expected to sell at $\frac{1}{8}$% pa above LIBOR, the lead manager could afford to set the yield at which it purchased notes from the borrower at $\frac{1}{4}$% pa above LIBOR, thereby assuring itself of a $\frac{1}{8}$% pa turn and the issuer of a $\frac{1}{8}$% pa overall cost saving.

There are two further important factors to recognise in this groundbreaking transaction. First, Citicorp acted as the sole placing agent for all the notes issued under this facility. We shall see later how this role of controlling the distribution of notes became pivotal and highly contentious especially when other banks were participating as underwriters in the same facility. Second, in selling the notes purchased from the issuer, Citicorp would have succeeded in removing the transaction from its balance sheet. As lending margins continued to decline, return on assets became an increasingly important (perhaps the most important) measure of profitability for banks and the focus shifted inexorably away from on-balance sheet interest-differential business to off-balance sheet, fee- or commission-generating business. Both these points will be amplified in later chapters but we should recognise in them themes which had important influences on the crystallisation of a true Euro-commercial paper market a few years later.

The New Zealand Shipping Corporation transaction did not enjoy exhaustive publicity at the time. This was in part due to the desire to keep an innovative and profitable business structure proprietary – always an immensely difficult task in the Euromarkets. It may also have been due to the recognition that this structure disintermediated commercial banks in their traditional short- *and* medium-term lending business. US banks, especially, had seen their domestic lending business with major corporates decimated by the rise of the domestic commercial paper market and the prospect of a re-occurrence in the Euro-markets was not greeted with much approbation. Obviously a cautious and measured approach was adopted as no similar facilities, according to publicised records, were signed in 1979. In 1980 a number were signed including Total Marine Norsk A/S in January. Other bank competitors had learned the technique and, besides Citicorp, Credit Suisse First Boston Limited and Swiss Bank Corporation International Limited both lead-managed similar facilities in 1980. However, the landmark transaction which deservedly earned extraordinary publicity occurred in April 1981 and it was once again a New Zealand borrower which took the lead. In this case, the government itself, Her Majesty in Right of New Zealand, was the borrower. Once again Citicorp was the arranger.

The facility was called a euronote issuance facility and totalled $500 million with a final maturity of seven years. Although very similar to the note purchase facility it differed from the New Zealand Shipping Corporation transaction in one fundamental way. The ten banks which provided the credit back-up – called the 'underwriters' – were each permitted to purchase euronotes at the contractual margin above LIBOR up to the amount of their individual commitments. Furthermore, each bank was unrestricted as to where it could sell those euronotes it had purchased and each retained the turn made on any sale. Should a bank be unable to sell some or all of the euronotes it had purchased, then it held them for its own account, effectively a loan on its balance sheet. The important variation therefore was the absence of an exclusive right of the arranger/lead manager to place all the euronotes issued under the facility. The obvious benefit to the issuer was the necessarily wider distribution of euronotes assured by having ten placing banks rather than one. The participating banks had a secure supply of euronotes with which to develop their own investor network and this too would become a frequently heard argument in ensuing years as different euronote distribution techniques were developed.

There are a number of other reasons why the New Zealand transaction was such a milestone. As the largest facility of its genre so far, it dwarfed its antecedents which were typically for $100 million or less. Not only was size a factor but so too credit quality; the borrower was one of the strongest sovereign credits available and its business highly sought after by international banks. Furthermore the facility was syndicated amongst an equally high quality group of banks, most of which were active in the Euro-securities market and had pretensions to develop their own euronote placement activities. It was no surprise therefore that it seized public attention; nor that the structure and pricing became common knowledge and legitimised in the market. The apparent cost savings made it an essential borrowing option for top quality borrowers to consider and there would be no shortage of banks bringing it to their attention.

Table 1

Euronote issuance facilities

VOLUME AND NUMBER OF TRANSACTIONS 1978–1983

Year	Volume (US $m)	Number of transactions
1978	30	1
1979	–	–
1980	278	6
1981	1822	21
1982	3185	26
1983	3547	30

Source: Euromoney

Exploitation of the new financing technique was much more rapid after the New Zealand transaction in 1981 than it was after the New Zealand Shipping Corporation transaction in 1978. Table 1 above shows that no similar facilities were publicly signed in 1979 whereas 1981 saw a 600% increase over the volume of facilities arranged in the previous three years together. The following two years, 1982 and 1983, saw 56 transactions, exactly double the number previously arranged. Volume too soared with over $3 billion of transactions arranged in each of those years.

Closer examination, however, affords some interesting observations on the direction this rapid growth was taking. We observed that after the New Zealand Shipping Corporation transaction no proliferation of the borrowing structure occurred out of a desire to keep it proprietary and, probably more importantly, because of banks' resistance to the disintermediation effect on their traditional lending business to corporate customers. It was not widely marketed to corporate borrowers. Table 2 below shows that in 1981 the note purchase facility was not a product aimed at banks' corporate customers with only $270 million in facilities arranged and these comprised only four facilities, of which two were for the Mexican subsidiaries of US industrial companies.

For the next two years after the New Zealand transaction corporate borrowers increased their activity but were still not the major factor in the euronote issuance facility market. From a meagre 15% of a small market in 1981 corporate borrowers took their share up to 30% in 1982, equalling

Table 2

Euronote issuance facilities

VOLUME (US$M) AND NUMBER OF TRANSACTIONS BY TYPE OF BORROWER 1978–83

	1978/79	1980	1981	1982	1983
Sovereign	30 (1)	50 (1)	700 (2)	950 (2)	50 (1)
Supranational	–	100 (1)	–	150 (2)	–
Corporate	–	30 (1)	270 (4)	980 (8)	809 (8)
Bank	–	98 (3)	852 (15)	1105 (14)	2688 (21)
TOTAL	30 (1)	278 (6)	1822 (21)	3185 (26)	3547 (30)

Source: Euromoney

sovereign borrowers in the US dollar volume of facilities arranged. This they maintained in 1983 whilst sovereign borrowers, inexplicably, fell to practically zero. A few corporate borrowers of excellent standing also started to use this market: Renault, AB Volvo, Alcoa, CRA. Whilst it may be argued that commercial banks were successful in protecting their corporate lending business, this is not a wholly satisfactory answer to the relatively small interest shown by corporates in this market. It is especially unsatisfactory if we take into account the fact that commercial bank lending was increasingly considered an unattractive business since fierce competition and excessive liquidity were causing continuous downward pressure on lending margins and a deterioration in return on assets ratios. Investment banks with no commercial lending business to protect were naturally eager to develop the product in order to break profitably into that business and they marketed euronote issuance facilities heavily to borrowers of all types. The answer probably lies more in the conservatism of the corporate borrower and its less regular funding needs compared to sovereign and bank borrowers. In order to sell their euronotes to investors, borrowers needed to be of undoubted quality and the number of corporate borrowers in this category was thus necessarily restricted. Before they would risk their name in a relatively untested market many chose to adopt a 'wait and see' attitude and to enter the market when it had matured and proved itself a viable alternative.

Banks and, to a lesser extent, sovereign borrowers took a different, more opportunistic approach. The latter had large development programmes or balance of payments deficits to finance. The former had significant wholesale funding needs and were always interested in accessing new and cheaper sources of finance. Both had a need to experiment and Table 2 above amply demonstrates their domination through to 1983, jointly accounting for 84% of market volume and 73% of total transactions by 1983.

The euronote issuance facility market grew from a $30 million facility arranged in 1978 to over $3 billion in 30 facilities in 1983. Whether this can be truly called the 'euronote' market is a moot point since statistical evidence as to how many of the borrowers were actually issuing euronotes is virtually non-existent and we must rely on educated guesswork. Clearly, there was nowhere near $3 billion worth of euronotes in issue since most facilities had been arranged as standby facilities, at cheap cost, to be used only when other funding sources either dried up or became too expensive. It must be remembered that domestic commercial paper still represented for most borrowers the cheapest source of short-term US dollar finance. The actual volume of outstandings of euronotes was probably well under $1 billion and perhaps even nearer to $500m.

BANK ISSUERS

What is more important to focus on at this time is the proportion of bank issuers which rose consistently from 1980 onwards: from three in 1980 to 21 in 1983 representing an increase in volume from $98 million to $2,688 million. The combined volume of bank transactions by 1983 was almost US$ 5 billion. Since there are no reliable statistics about how much paper was actually in issue it is impossible to track investor preferences as to bank, corporate or sovereign paper. The nomenclature of the market changed somewhat and, instead of the note purchase facility, the CD-issuance facility proliferated, Credit Suisse First Boston Limited and Merrill Lynch International Bank Limited becoming two of the most active arrangers of such facilities.

There are a number of reasons for the sudden increase in the number of CD-issuance facilities for banks. Each of them has a degree of relevance though each on its own cannot claim to be the dominant reason for this increase. One factor which will become increasingly important later in the development of Euro-commercial paper is the effect on major, particularly US, banks of the Latin American debt crisis and serious deterioration in certain domestic US industry sectors. Mexico's moratorium on its debt servicing in August 1982 and massive loan exposures to other developing countries along with the especially troubled US domestic energy sector meant substantially increased non-performing loans, write-offs and plummetting earnings for several large commercial banks during the period 1982–4. This seriously affected investors' perception of the risk of the commercial bank sector, particularly in the US, and certain banks' cost of funds increased as a result of investors' flight into more secure, higher quality instruments. The differential between three-month Euro-CDs and three-month US Treasury Bills in mid-1984 when the crisis was perhaps at its zenith widened to about 2% (see Tables 3 and 4 below). For Continental Illinois National Bank and Trust Company of Chicago and its holding company Continental Illinois Corporation it became a question of not at what rate funds could be raised but whether funds could be raised at all. In what was one of the most dramatic events in banking history, Continental Illinois, one of the largest banks in the world, faced substantial withdrawals of funds by depositors in May 1984 and had to agree a rescue plan with US Federal regulators in July 1984. Without the restructuring plan of the Federal Deposit Insurance Corporation, the Federal Reserve and the Comptroller of the Currency it is doubtful whether investors in Continental Illinois' paper would have been repaid. Whilst Continental Illinois' depositors did not lose money, investors in bank risk instruments were profoundly shaken by the size, speed and scope of the crisis.

A total of 35 banks, of which nine were money-centre and large regional banks, suffered a downgrading of their long-term debt ratings by Standard & Poor's in 1983, with particular activity in the last half of that year. Whilst the

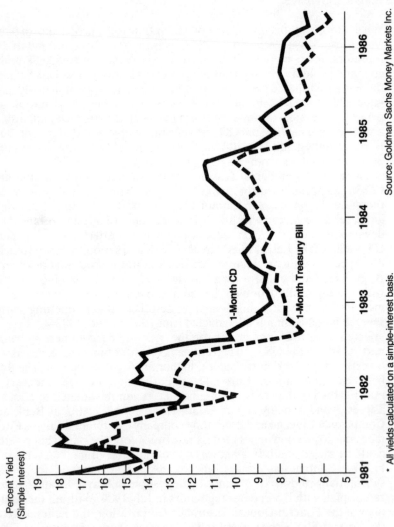

Table 3   **Historical Interest Rate Comparison** *

30-Day Maturity

Percent Yield
(Simple Interest)

1-Month CD

1-Month Treasury Bill

1981 1982 1983 1984 1985 1986

* All yields calculated on a simple-interest basis.

Source: Goldman Sachs Money Markets Inc.

Table 4

Historical Interest Rate Comparison*
90-Day Maturity

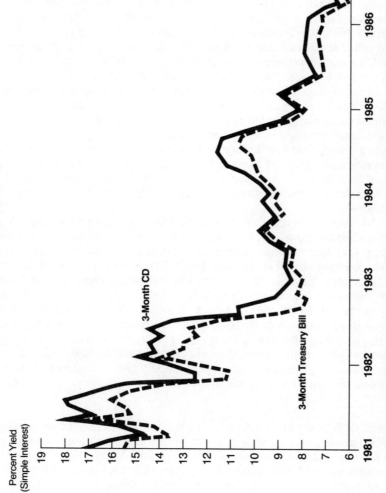

Percent Yield
(Simple Interest)

3-Month CD

3-Month Treasury Bill

1981 1982 1983 1984 1985 1986

* All yields calculated on a simple-interest basis.

Source: Goldman Sachs Money Markets Inc.

figures also account for 20 upgradings closer analysis shows that these were largely for consumer finance companies such as Associates Corporation of North America and Chrysler Financial Corporation. This trend continued into 1984 with a further 32 bank downgradings including some of the largest US bank holding companies. Only two AAA ratings were reaffirmed in a January 1984 review of the financial sector. Foreign banks were not exempt from the analysts' scrutiny since they too were suffering from the same Latin American debt problems as their US counterparts and several could not escape the downgrading of certain of their public debt issues. Banque Nationale de Paris, Barclays North American Capital Corporation, Long Term Credit Bank of Japan, National Westminster Bank Limited, all had issues downgraded by Standard & Poor's from AAA in 1984. The following year saw no respite with 40 US financial institution downgradings, attributable to weakness additionally in the real estate and agricultural sectors of the US economy.

For a number of weeks at the height of the Continental Illinois crisis the effect was to cause real doubt in investors' minds about the security of even the largest commercial banks. These banks weathered that particular storm but the experience focussed investors' attention on not only the size of the problems facing many of the world's largest banks but on how quickly these problems can develop and get out of hand. If large banks were still a relatively secure risk, they nonetheless had caused investors to challenge the conventional wisdom that making a time-deposit or buying bank CDs was the investment route of least risk.

Whether it was the growing doubts and uncertainties over the US 'money-centre' banks from 1982–84 which caused investors to switch a proportion of their investments into certificates of deposit issued by more secure, less exposed banks or whether some banks felt it prudent to establish committed CD-issuance facilities in case funding became difficult for all banks, it is impossible to determine precisely. Both are true to varying degrees. Nevertheless the number of euronote issuance facilities arranged by financial institutions more than doubled from 15 in 1981 to 32 in 1984 making an aggregate total of 85 for that four-year period. It was noticeable at the time by those working in the euronote market (although statistical evidence is, as ever, poor) that a higher volume of paper was being issued and more investors were buying the instrument for the first time.

Looking back over this period from 1983 it is evident that the concept originally called a note purchase facility had become a well-established banking product. It took on a variety of names as different banks discovered and used it for their own customers: CD-issuance facility, note issuance facility, euronote purchase agreement, euronote issuance facility or revolving underwriting facility. The variation in product description could not mask its simple structural theme, namely that commercial banks (or underwriters as they were most often called) provided the borrower with credit insurance for the required period in the 'back-stop' commitment and borrowings were effected through the issuance of euronotes or certificates of deposit. For ease of reference we will use the term 'euronote issuance facility' for the remainder of this book.

However, if the concept behind the various facility names was uniform, there were differences apparent in the methods of distributing the notes under these facilities. We have seen how in the New Zealand Shipping Corporation transaction Citicorp had the sole right to place notes – although this was somewhat logical since it was the only bank providing the credit back-stop.

In the large New Zealand transaction each bank providing the credit back-stop was permitted to place euronotes up to the amount of its own commitment. It was Merrill Lynch International Bank Limited which brought further innovation to distribution methods in syndicated transactions it arranged, by playing the role of the 'sole placing agent'. The key difference was that Merrill Lynch had the exclusive right to place all euronotes issued under a facility where the credit back-stop was provided by a separate group of (usually) commercial banks. If the sole placing agent was unable to place euronotes, then the underwriting banks purchased them at a pre-agreed, contractual margin above LIBOR. Thus the sole placing agent earned all the potential sales commissions whilst the underwriting banks played the passive role of credit back-stop for which they earned an annual fee. We shall analyse this method fully in the next chapter.

From 1981 onwards, therefore, the market had accepted a new borrowing structure and it was to undergo some considerable developmental changes in the light of a number of key trends:

– increasingly fierce competition between banks for borrower mandates
– a continuing decline in lending margins
– general nervousness about the creditworthiness of the commercial bank sector, particularly the money-centre banks
– a preoccupation with, and ultimately disagreement over, the optimal euronote distribution technique.

We shall analyse in detail in the next chapter the numerous euronote distribution methods which followed the New Zealand transaction in the years 1981–4. In chapter 5 we will analyse in detail the Euro-commercial paper programme as it became properly established in 1985. However, in order to maintain correct chronology and review parallel developments as they occur, it must be mentioned that the Euro-commercial paper programme appeared once again during this period when euronote issuance facilities were capturing most of the headlines.

A SECOND ATTEMPT AT EURO-COMMERCIAL PAPER

In late 1980 while the New Zealand transaction was being planned and organised, the first Euro-commercial paper programmes since the OFDI-related programmes of the early 1970s appeared. It was Merrill Lynch International Bank Limited alone which attempted to re-establish the structure in the Euromarkets. It arranged two such programmes – called 'Euro Commercial Paper Notes' – for Associates Corporation of North America and IC Industries, both US companies which already had domestic commercial paper programmes.

Associates Corporation of North America ('Associates') was at the time the seventh largest independent finance company in the US measured by total capital funds and in 1979 had begun consumer finance operations in Japan and the UK. It was (and is) a subsidiary of Gulf & Western Industries Inc and in its own right at the time was rated A on its long-term debt and A1P1 on its commercial paper. The $100 million programme constituted senior unsecured debt and was established on the domestic model in that it was a best efforts, uncommitted programme with Merrill Lynch acting in an agency role as a dealer whose responsibility was the placement of the notes. Strategically the programme was designed as a means of diversifying Associates' funding sources at a time of commercial expansion into overseas markets. The company actually required sterling financing in the UK and, since it was not permitted to issue sterling commercial paper, it used the US dollars generated by the programme to swap into sterling through the foreign exchange markets. The notes were priced at US dollar LIBOR plus 0.125% pa at a time when commercial bank credit lines were generally being offered at LIBOR plus 0.50–0.75% pa. Depending on the conditions prevailing in the foreign exchange markets at the time of issuing notes, Associates' cost of sterling was around sterling LIBOR plus 0.125%. Another reason for attempting to establish a Euro-commercial paper market was the ability to find investors which typically invested for maturities of 90 to 180 days, longer than the domestic commercial paper average which was closer to 30 days. This financing source provided therefore a potentially complementary maturity range.

From an operational viewpoint the notes were bearer instruments issued at a discount in denominations of minimum $500,000 rising by $100,000 increments. LIBOR would be fixed at 11.00 am two days prior to issue date. Merrill Lynch itself organised the issuing and paying agency function and investors were issued with definitive bearer notes (see example below). A short information circular accompanied the programme and gave the following information:

  (i) summary of terms of the notes;
 (ii) use of proceeds;
(iii) form of the notes;
(iv) a description of Associates; and
 (v) selected financial data of Associates.

The circular was designed to give investors basic quantitative and qualitative information on which to form the credit decision whether to invest in the notes or not.

Associates' experience of the programme was positive and it became the company's most cost-effective source of sterling finance. However, the programme was not used to its fullest extent, with about $5–10m outstanding at one time and $50m raised overall. The company did diversify its source of funds managing to attract investing institutions such as insurance companies and investment trusts. The relatively small amount issued should not be taken to mean that the notes were unattractive to investors nor that the market was non-existent. Rather the commercial banks' response to the programme had the most important bearing on how much it was used – just as we saw in the early programmes six or seven years before. Banks, quite simply, lowered their pricing on credit facilities more out of general market competition than a

Specimen note from Associates Corporation of North America's Euro-commercial paper programme (1980)

ASSOCIATES CORPORATION OF NORTH AMERICA

1 Gulf + Western Plaza, New York, New York 10023

No. P **000000**

19

U.S. $ [box]

On _____ Associates Corporation of North America for value received hereby promises irrevocably and unconditionally to pay to the bearer on surrender of this Note (a) at the principal office of Merrill Lynch International Bank Limited in London, England, or (b) at the office of Merrill Lynch International Bank Limited or its designated agent in New York City, the principal sum of

_____ United States dollars. Payment at the office referred to in (a) above will be made in New York Clearing House funds by check or draft drawn on, or by telegraphic transfer through, a bank in New York City.

Associates Corporation of North America also will pay to the bearer of this Note such amount as may be necessary so that payment to such bearer, net of all taxes, assessments or other governmental charges imposed by or required to be withheld from such payment by the United States of America, will not be less than the amount provided for herein at the time such amount is due and payable.

This Note is governed by and is to be construed in accordance with the laws of the State of New York.

ASSOCIATES CORPORATION OF NORTH AMERICA

By _____
                              Authorized Signature

Countersigned, without recourse:
Merrill Lynch International Bank Limited

By _____
         Authorized Signature
Not Valid Unless Countersigned by Merrill Lynch International Bank Limited

This Note has not been registered under the Securities Act of 1933 of the United States of America. Any offer or sale of this Note in the United States (including its territories and possessions and all areas subject to its jurisdiction) or to nationals or residents thereof (including any corporation or other entity created or organized therein) may constitute a violation of United States laws unless such offer or sale is either registered pursuant to or is exempt from registration under or complies with the said Act.

No prospectus has been or will be registered in Great Britain in respect of this Note and, accordingly, it may not be offered in Great Britain except to persons whose ordinary business it is to buy or sell shares or debentures, whether as principal or agent.

SPECIMEN

specific reaction to the potential disintermediation. Over the two years to 1982 credit pricing dropped while the tone of the consumer finance industry improved, thus enabling Associates to command better terms on its bank loans and therefore to discontinue the Euro-commercial paper programme.

Very few programmes followed those of Associates and IC Industries. The environment had proved relatively favourable to the sale of euronotes of sovereign issuers such as New Zealand but perhaps less so for corporate issuers. That is not to say that corporate issuers were of poor quality, the contrary is in fact true. It is more to do with the attitude of the investor. Hitherto investors had almost exclusively invested in short-term bank risk, mainly time-deposits and CDs. Innovations such as euronotes evidencing indebtedness of a non-bank entity took time to be understood and accepted. Thus in the 1980–82 period banks were faced with the task of persuading investors of the merits of investing in euronotes and were having to overcome traditional conservatism as well as the inertia of established investment procedures. Not only did investors have to understand the instrument but they were being asked to assess the credit of a non-bank obligor. In the case of major sovereign credits this was a relatively straightforward risk to evaluate but it was not at all easy in the case of corporates. The US credit ratings meant relatively little since ratings in general were not a feature of the short-term money markets outside the US. Investors were obviously attracted by a higher yield on euronotes than on deposits but, since investing in bank risk was procedurally simple and considered extremely safe,[1] those yields generally had to be well above LIBOR to attract investors. Most investors at this time required a yield enhancement of between 0.125% p a and 0.375% p a to invest in euronotes. In most cases, therefore, investors were commercial banks looking for opportunistic assets which they could match fund and lock in an attractive margin.

Only two programmes of an uncommitted nature similar to that of Associates appeared before 1984: the Republic of South Africa (October 1981); and the Australian Resources Development Bank Limited (ARDB) (October 1983). Both were arranged by Swiss Bank Corporation International Limited (SBCI),[2] and both were best efforts programmes aimed at developing an investor base for the notes of both issuers.

The ARDB programme for example is issuer-led with ARDB requesting to issue a series of notes (actually CDs) of a specific amount and maturity. SBCI, the dealer, allows itself two days to consult with several of its investors and at the end of a minimum two-day period it quotes a yield (relative to LIBOR) at which it will purchase the series of notes on offer. ARBD has a further day to accept or reject the dealer's quotation. Once accepted, the dealer is at risk on the paper at the quoted yield. The programme, whilst not as time-efficient as present-day programmes, nevertheless boasts their basic strengths. The issuer and dealer can consult at will and advice is given about the amount and

1 It can be argued that investors considered bank risk safe but did not understand it. The banking crisis of 1983 onwards came as a shock to many large investors, especially the speed at which bank creditworthiness can deteriorate.
2 The Republic of Ireland arranged a similar facility in March 1982 but since it was connected with a committed facility it does not come within the strict definition of a Euro-commercial paper programme.

maturity of notes most appropriate for market conditions. The dealer quotes for the notes in relation to investor demand and thus the pricing mechanism is market-related. Certain features such as offering a fixed tranche of notes of a single maturity are borrowed from the euronote issuance facility though taken as a whole the programme was a genuine forerunner of the present type of Euro-commercial paper programme.

CHAPTER 3

Syndicated facility structures and distribution techniques

It is not the intention of this book to analyse the loan syndication process but we will examine that process in so far as it affected the facility structures and techniques adopted for the distribution of euronotes. Most obviously, of course, as transactions grew in size or were arranged by investment banks which could not or would not provide the credit back-stop, euronote issuance facilities had to be syndicated amongst several commercial banks. The fact that these were syndicated rather than one-on-one facilities became critical. Winning mandates is a function not only of price, but also of structure. Arrangers of euronote issuance facilities found it increasingly difficult to attract banks to underwrite facilities on the simple transaction economics and in order to ensure successful syndication were obliged to amend facility structures to offer banks potentially improved economics such as access to euronotes which they could sell and generate additional earnings. Such amendments had also to provide demonstrable benefits to an issuer about to give its mandate. Such benefits and improved economics were sometimes a chimera to banks and issuers alike.

Let us now examine in detail the various facility structures and the distribution methods used from the beginning of this market. Both the New Zealand Shipping Corporation and New Zealand transactions adopted the same distribution structure though the latter was syndicated amongst ten banks and the former was underwritten by a single bank. The price of the euronote was not related to investor demand but, paradoxically, to the cost of the committed back-stop facility. In both transactions the underwriting banks purchased euronotes at a fixed price contracted in the facility agreement – in the case of New Zealand (LIBOR plus ¼% pa). Each bank could choose either to hold the euronotes on its books, thereby effectively making a loan to the borrower, or it could on-sell the euronotes to investors at a lower yield, thereby taking the loan off its books and keeping the sales turn.

Taking the example of the New Zealand facility we can analyse the returns that this structure afforded the underwriting banks. The essential details of the facility are as follows:

Example 1

Amount:	$500 million
Maturity:	7 years
Maximum margin at which underwriting banks will purchase euronotes from New Zealand	LIBOR + 0.25% pa

Commitment fee: 0.25% pa payable on the
                                              undrawn amount of the
                                              commitment
10 underwriting banks: 4 at $75 million each
                                              2 at $50 million each
                                              4 at $25 million each

(a) If the facility were fully drawn throughout its life, the return on assets to each bank would be a straightforward 0.25% pa above LIBOR since the commitment fee would not be paid.

(b) If the facility were 50% drawn throughout its life, the return to each bank would actually double, ie to 0.50%. The simple arithmetic of this is as follows, taking a bank with $75 million commitment:

$37,500,000 outstanding at ¼% margin   = $93,750
¼% pa commitment fee on $37,500,000   = $93,750
                                                      ————————
                                                      $187,500

Loans outstanding (ie assets) of $37,500,000

Return on assets   = $\frac{187,500 \times 100}{37,500,000}$

                                              =   0.50% pa

(c) If the facility were entirely undrawn, then the 0.25% pa commitment fee would accrue over the life of the facility and hence the return on assets would be infinite because no assets would be recorded on the books of any bank.

Now, since each bank in any issue request by the borrower must purchase euronotes, it can on-sell them to investors and thereby enhance its return on assets. For example, in (b) above the bank has purchased from the issuer $37,500,000 of euronotes at ¼% pa above LIBOR. If it on-sells the euronotes at ⅛% pa above LIBOR it earns in a full year $46,875 ($37,500,000 × ⅛% pa) but loses the benefit of the margin income, ie $93,750. Though its earnings fall by half it succeeds in removing a loan from its balance sheet. With no asset recorded in its books the bank has an infinite return on assets! Many banks were prepared to accept an earnings reduction if it afforded an increased return on assets. However, they often began to write larger volumes of such underwriting business in order to restore earnings to former levels.

Only a modicum of perspicacity is required to see the glaring anomaly in this type of calculation of return on assets. In no circumstances does the underlying back-stop commitment which each bank legally carries throughout the seven years of the facility figure as a balance sheet item and hence include itself in the return on assets calculation. If the facility were undrawn or the euronotes all sold to investors banks acted as though the commitment did not exist. The concept of risk asset only applied if an actual loan were being made. If the investor market for short-term euronotes dried up for whatever reason, the underwriting banks would still be obliged to purchase euronotes from the borrower and thus create an asset on their balance sheets. In fairness, some banks conservatively applied a balance sheet value to the underlying commitment and their decisions as to pricing were guided accordingly; others did not and began to write significant volumes of this business with small regard for the capital implications. We shall see in 1985 and, especially, in 1986 how central bank regulators sought to apply sensible guidelines on euronote issuance facilities and to bring such commitments into a bank's return on assets calculation.

However, during the explosive growth period of euronote issuance facilities from 1984 onwards (see Table 10, below), conversion of loan interest income into fee income through securitising debt in euronote form and selling it to investors became critical to banks which found absolute pricing levels and the resulting return on assets unattractive. Many banks rationalised that a facility designed only to be a back-up or standby facility and thus not intended to be drawn was excellent business since the commitment fee could merely be credited to fee income and, since it was probable that no euronotes would ever be held on the books, the return on assets would be infinite. This was and still is a dangerous assumption since it is exposed to the risk that other financial markets, including the euronote market, become closed to that issuer and the standby facility has to be activated.

One of the essential attractions of the New Zealand facility was that it enabled each underwriting bank to obtain a supply of euronotes on which it had the opportunity to generate fee income and to develop its own investor clientele. An alternative structure was being promoted at the same time which in this respect was crucially different and it became known as the revolving underwriting facility (RUF) using the sole placing agency distribution method.

SOLE PLACING AGENCY

Merrill Lynch International Bank Limited became closely associated with this structure and promoted it very successfully from about 1981 onwards. The first sole placing agency RUF was a $30m, six-year transaction arranged by Merrill Lynch for Banco Totta y Acores (London Branch) and signed on 29 June 1981.

It is quite simple in concept and structure and the essential difference from a note purchase facility is that, instead of the underwriting banks purchasing the euronotes from the issuer and on-selling or holding them, a sole placing agent (usually, the arranger) has the exclusive right to sell the euronotes to investors. In the facility agreement a contractual margin above LIBOR is established and this is known, when taken with LIBOR, as the 'maximum interest rate' and represents the maximum cost the issuer can pay. It is also simply referred to as the 'cap rate'. Euronotes cannot be bought from the issuer by the sole placing agent at a rate higher than the cap rate. In the event that the sole placing agent cannot sell any or all of the euronotes into the market the underwriting banks are obliged to purchase unsold euronotes at the cap rate. The underwriting banks thus play a passive role as providers of credit insurance and rely for their ultimate return on assets entirely on the placement capabilities of the sole placing agent as well as the condition of the market for short-term debt securities.

The underwriting banks are paid a 'facility fee' or an 'underwriting fee', quarterly or semi-annually in arrear each year, for the provision of the credit insurance. This is their only remuneration (besides usually a small one-off participation fee at the time of syndication). Unlike a commitment fee in a revolving credit facility which is paid on the undrawn amount of the commitment, the facility fee is paid irrespective of the utilisation of the facility. Generally speaking, this fee when added to the cap rate produces an overall return commensurate with what would be payable as a margin on the borrower's straightforward revolving credit facility (or, in fact, lower since continuously declining credit pricing meant that a new facility would be cheaper than the old one). For example, if a simple revolving credit facility is priced at:

(a) Interest rate: LIBOR + 0.25% pa
     Commitment fee: 0.125% pa

the return, if the facility is fully drawn, is 0.25% pa above LIBOR and, if always undrawn, 0.125% pa.

Similarly if a euronote issuance facility is priced at:

(b) Cap rate: LIBOR + 0.125% pa
     Facility fee: 0.125% pa

the return fully drawn is 0.25% pa above LIBOR (the sum of the cap rate and the facility fee) and the return, if always undrawn, is 0.125%. The two methods produce the same drawn and undrawn returns but price the actual asset (advance or euronote) differently.

Unlike the New Zealand transaction the price of the euronote for the issuer in a sole placing agency RUF is not *wholly* related to the market price of the credit back-stop. Because the facility fee is payable irrespective of the facility's utilisation, the margin above LIBOR on the euronote is, as we have seen, lower than the margin payable on a normal medium-term credit facility. Indeed, the margin on the euronote should be somewhat above the maximum investors would expect to receive for the issuer's short-term debt obligations and the sum of the facility fee and any other fees payable (such as one-off participation fees) should be so geared as to bring the combined total margin up to the medium-term credit pricing expected of the issuer in the market. Thus the built-in profit for the sole placing agent in a RUF is less than that for the banks in a New Zealand-type transaction, ie there is a larger sales turn in a facility priced as (a) above rather than (b). Although the price of the euronote for the issuer in a sole placing agency RUF is not wholly related to the price of the credit back-stop, it is not yet wholly divorced from it.

The margin above LIBOR on the euronotes is established both as a function of the present market for the issuer's short-term debt obligations as well as an estimation of the future market. Banks would not be willing to underwrite if they felt the cap rate was not sufficiently high to accommodate a market increase in short-term lending margins during the life of the facility without incurring an opportunity loss on a committed facility of this type.

Let us examine how in practice an issue of euronotes under the sole placing agency method works.

Example 2

Issuer:	SPA Corporation
Amount:	US$ 100 million
Maturity of facility:	7 years
Issue of euronotes:	$25 million of 3-month euronotes
Cap rate:	0.125% p a above LIBOR
Underwriting banks:	10 each with $10 million commitment
Underwriting fee:	0.125% p a

Typically, SPA Corporation will give five business days' notice to the agent that it wishes to issue $25 million of three-month euronotes. That is to say, it requires funds in its bank account with good value in five days' time. The underwriting banks are similarly advised of this issue request so that they can be prepared for the possible purchase of euronotes. The sole placing agent will now have a maximum three-day selling period during which it seeks investors to purchase up to $25 million of three-month notes at a yield at or below three-month LIBOR plus 0.125% p a (the cap rate). Of course, in order to make a turn it will need to sell euronotes *below* the cap rate. If the sole placing agent succeeds in selling all the euronotes to investors at LIBOR plus 0.10% p a, it will have thus earned a sales turn of 0.025% p a which equates to:

$$\$25,000,000 \times 0.025\% \times \frac{90}{360}$$
$$= \$1,562.50$$

If, however, the sole placing agent is able to sell only $10 million of euronotes at LIBOR plus 0.10% p a it will then notify the underwriting banks that it requires a total of $15 million of euronotes to be purchased by them at the maximum interest rate of LIBOR plus 0.125% p a. This purchase obligation is executed pro-rata to the banks' commitments in the facility. In this example, $15 million is divided between ten banks each having a $10 million commitment and thus each bank is obliged to purchase $1.5 million of euronotes. The sole placing agent has still earned a sales turn of 0.025% on the $10 million of euronotes it actually sold, i e $625.

The underwriting banks are notified of their allocation of euronotes prior to the setting of LIBOR to allow them to consider their options as to funding the asset with a matching liability or to mismatch their funding in order potentially to enhance their earnings. The underwriting banks are not themselves constrained from selling the euronotes subsequently to investors should they be able to find demand. However, with a skilled and hard-working sole placing agent it is unlikely, although not impossible, that underwriting banks will find many opportunities to place unsold notes they have been obliged to purchase.

Table 5

Typical timetable for sole placing agency procedure

Issue date minus 5 days:	Sole placing agent receives by 11.00 am from the issuer a request to issue euronotes, specifying the US dollar amount, the issue date and maturity.
Issue date minus 4 days:	Sole placing agent informs the underwriting bank of the details of the issue request.
Issue date minus 5 days to minus 2 days:	Selling period during which the sole placing agent offers euronotes to investors.
Issue date minus 2 days:	A. Sole placing agent notifies the underwriting banks by telephone (and subsequently by telex) of any amount of euronotes remaining unsold and requiring to be purchased by the underwriting banks. B. Relevant LIBOR is set about 11.00 am by 2 or 3 reference banks (the issuing agent can also act as reference agent for this purpose). C. Sole placing agent notifies issuing agent of the details of the issue.
Issue date:	A. The issuing agent authenticates the euronotes. B. Proceeds of the sale of euronotes are to be paid by either the underwriting banks or investors into the issuer's New York bank account by 10.00 am (New York time). Either sole placing agent or issuing agent may act as collecting bank for these funds. C. The issuing agent delivers the euronotes to the sole placing agent or to its order.

The overall period between issue request and receipt of funds can vary from case to case and, indeed, early facilities provided for as much as ten days.

It has been stated that a critical difference between a sole placing agency revolving underwriting facility and the New Zealand-type note purchase facility is that the latter allows banks to share the euronote placement earnings whilst the former does not. It would be useful to examine how important these earnings are, especially in relation to the underwriting fee or facility fee earned by the back-stop banks.

Taking again Example 2 above, the back-stop banks earn an underwriting fee of 0.125% pa. For a bank with a commitment of $10 million this is equivalent to $12,500 per annum. The sole placing agent, we have seen, has the exclusive opportunity to exceed these earnings provided the facility is extensively used and demand in the short-term securities market remains positive. If the facility is fully drawn the sole placing agent can earn $12,500 in one year by placing all the euronotes at a turn of 0.0125% p a, ie 1.25 basis points. Under market conditions as they have existed hitherto, the sales turn would generally be in excess of 0.0125% p a and in any case would tend to increase over time as short-term lending margins continued to decline and as investors became used to the issuer's name and accepted lower yields. In some instances, perhaps in many, a turn of 0.0625% p a would not be unrealistic. At that level in the above facility, if fully drawn, the sole placing agent would earn $62,500, five times the annual earnings of each underwriting bank.

There were justificatory reasons for this potential imbalance of earnings with the sole placing agent arguing that its skill and reputation as a placer of euronotes was continuously under review in the sales process and that it had a continuing obligation to perform well in good and bad markets alike. Nevertheless it is hardly surprising that pressure mounted for a structure which allowed underwriting banks to participate more fully in the placement of euronotes and to allow them a potential share of these placement earnings. Some banks claimed that as they were taking all the credit risk, these earnings were rightfully theirs, ignoring the fact that the underwriting fee was meant to cover this aspect. A structure did appear, known as the euronote issuance facility with a tender panel. Perhaps more importantly, issuers saw the opportunity to share in these placement earnings themselves by trying to reduce them through relating more exactly the margin payable on any offering of euronotes (ie their borrowing cost) to the market price for short-term securities rather than the market price of the back-stop facility. This would represent an important step away from the sole placing agency RUF.

TENDER PANEL

This is a distribution technique which was first used in the market in 1982. The technique is alleged to have been borrowed from the Australian financial market, a view supported by the fact that the first three borrowers to use it were all Australian. There is some contention as to the first issuer. In 1982 there were two facilities using the tender panel structure, MIM Holdings Limited (guaranteed by Mount Isa Mines Limited) and CRA Finance Limited (guaranteed by CRA Limited) both arranged by BankAmerica International Group. Both facilities actually involved the issuance of a long-term euronote which investors on any interest payment date (every three or six months) could sell back to the underwriting banks. Investors, therefore, could effectively buy a three- or six-month risk instrument. Euronotes sold back by investors were offered to a tender panel comprising 24 banks in the MIM facility and 33 banks in the CRA facility. The first tender panel for conventional short-term euronotes was arranged by Credit Suisse First Boston Limited for the Australian Wheat Board in a $50m facility signed in August 1983.

Let us first examine the structure of the tender panel. It is merely a method of distribution of euronotes and does not really affect the basic structure of a euronote issuance facility. In addition to the group of underwriting banks in the facility a second group of banks skilled in the placement of euronotes is assembled; they need not have any underwriting commitment in the facility. This second group constitutes the tender panel and when the issuer requests an issue of euronotes it will ask, through a tender agent, the tender panel members to bid in auction for those euronotes. They are not, however, obliged to bid. There is a cap rate (often called the 'maximum offering margin') above which bids will be declared invalid. Bids are awarded to successful tender panel members starting from the lowest yield upwards.

With reference to Table 6 below we can see how the tender panel process operates. Let us take an example:

Example 3

Issuer:	TP Corporation
Facility amount:	$200 million
Underwriting banks:	10 with $20 million commitment each
Tender panel banks:	14 (Bank A through Bank N)
Issue request;	$60 million of 6-month euronotes
Maximum offering margin:	0.125% above LIBOR.

The tender agent, often but not invariably, is the arranger of the facility and it plays a co-ordinating and administrative role between the issuer and tender panel members (for which it would receive a small fee, perhaps between $500 and $2,000 per tender depending on the size of the tender panel). In the above example the tender agent might have received by noon on the third day prior to issue date the following bids (tenders) from the tender panel banks:

Tender panel member	Tender amount	Tender yield
Bank D	$4,000,000	LIBOR flat
Bank A	$1,000,000	LIBOR flat
Bank I	$2,000,000	LIBOR flat
Bank B	$3,000,000	LIBOR + 0.01% p a
Bank C	$1,000,000	LIBOR + 0.01% p a
Bank G	$5,000,000	LIBOR + 0.02% p a
Bank B	$3,000,000	LIBOR + 0.02% p a
Bank I	$8,000,000	LIBOR + 0.03% p a
Bank M	$5,000,000	LIBOR + 0.039% p a
Bank N	$4,000,000	LIBOR + 0.04% p a
Bank G	$10,000,000	LIBOR + 0.05% p a
Bank M	$5,000,000	LIBOR + 0.059% p a
Bank H	$5,000,000	LIBOR + 0.0625% p a
Bank G	$7,000,000	LIBOR + 0.07% p a
Bank D	$5,000,000	LIBOR + 0.07% p a
Bank B	$10,000,000	LIBOR + 0.10% p a
Bank I	$8,000,000	LIBOR + 0.125% p a
Bank L	$14,000,000	LIBOR + 0.125% p a

No bids received from banks E, F, J, K.

The aggregate bids received total $100,000,000 whereas only $60,000,000 is actually required by the issuer. Bids are awarded in ascending order of yield starting, of course, with the lowest. In this example, the cut-off point for accepting bids is LIBOR plus 0.07% p a, the two bids after the $5,000,000 bid by Bank H. Up to and including Bank H's bid, the total of bids accepted is $56,000,000 and so it is impossible to accept in full both Bank G *and* Bank D's bids at LIBOR plus 0.07% p a otherwise the issuer would receive $68,000,000.

What would happen would be that $4,000,000 only would be accepted, divided on as equitable a basis as possible between both banks. Because Bank G originally bid more than Bank D probable acceptance would be $2,500,000 from Bank G and $1,500,000 from Bank D. The bids from Banks B, I and L would not be accepted since the $60,000,000 has now been satisfied. Four banks did not bid and this is a fairly common feature of tender panels. The issuer's average cost is LIBOR plus 0.0364% p a, about 0.09% below the maximum offering margin or cap rate.

A number of points are worth making in the above example to illustrate how banks approach tender panel bidding. There is no restriction on the number of bids a bank can make and it is common to see banks 'scatter' their bids, especially in the first few issues under a facility. This is an effective method of determining the level at which the issuer's euronotes will be successfully sold. We must remember that banks are told of their successful bid(s) but are not always informed of the average accepted bid yield. A single bid at LIBOR (such as Bank A's) is not effective in establishing the issuer's average accepted bid yield, especially as it is for a small amount and there is no higher bid attempting to establish a range. Bank G's approach is more sensible with three bids, LIBOR flat, LIBOR plus 0.05% p a and LIBOR plus 0.07% p a. It gains from this bidding pattern important market information since its last bid is only partially awarded and therefore must be at the highest accepted yield. Moreover Bank G's average cost of buying $17,500,000 of euronotes is LIBOR plus 0.043% p a whereas Bank D's is $5,500,000 at LIBOR plus 0.019%. Hence through more skilful bidding Bank G not only has greater profit potential than Bank D on its purchase of euronotes but for the next tender has the important knowledge of the last tender's cut-off point for accepted bids. At the next tender Bank G's tactic would be probably not to repeat the previous bid of LIBOR plus 0.02% p a though it might maintain a bid at the LIBOR plus 0.05% p a level in case the bidding overall became more competitive.

Another tactic used by bidding banks is to bid a yield 0.001% below the normal 'round-figure' bids'. Bank M does this in the above example with its bids of LIBOR plus 0.039% p a and LIBOR plus 0.059% p a. Recognising that most banks make 'round-figure' bids, this tactic will ensure that the slightly lower bid will be awarded should the two bids fall on the cut-off point. The winning bank will have its bid awarded at virtually no loss of profit potential since the cost of the 'odd-figure bid' is only $10 per $1,000,000.

From a practical point of view there are a number of problems with the tender panel process. The sheer size of some tender panels means that communication with the tender agent, and hence the issuer, can be difficult. With 30 or more tender panel members all sending in their bids by telex in the last hour or so before the deadline it is hardly surprising that some bids fail to arrive at the tender agent by that deadline due to telex traffic congestion. In the early days of what was a new product some banks' inexperience showed and bids above the maximum offering margin were quite regularly received. Bids with accidentally transposed figures (LIBOR plus 0.0125% pa instead of LIBOR plus 0.125%) caused some banks to be awarded euronotes at rock-bottom yields when they had in fact been bidding high in order not to obtain euronotes. With notice periods of over a week some banks quite simply filed the issue request and then forgot to bid. Some banks still have never submitted a bid despite having been a tender panel member for over two years!

ABSOLUTE RATE BIDDING

In most cases tender panel bidding is related to LIBOR or LIBID simply because of the time that the operational procedures require. Bids have to be tied to a benchmark that reflects changes in market interest rates otherwise the bidding banks would have to run an unacceptable interest rate risk. Some issuers included in their tender panel an option to receive absolute rate bids, ie bids expressed as a pure interest rate and not tied to the LIBOR or LIBID benchmark. It is necessary to compress the absolute rate bidding procedure into three days between issue request and receipt of funds. The actual period of time a bank's absolute rate bid is outstanding is usually about one and a half to two hours and for most banks this is unacceptably long, especially in a potentially volatile interest rate environment (though it must be said that most issuers would probably not use the absolute rate bidding procedure in such conditions). A period of 15 minutes or so is much preferred as the optimum period to have an absolute rate bid outstanding – clearly with upwards of a dozen tender panel members communication logistics means this is not feasible. Absolute rate bidding – whilst now the essence of the Euro-commercial paper programme – is not extensively used in tender panels. Table 7 below shows a typical timetable for absolute rate bidding.

Table 6

Timetable of an issue of euronotes through the tender panel process

Issue date minus 5 days:	A. Issuer sends a telex to the tender agent requesting an issue of euronotes, specifying: (i) the US dollar amount required; (ii) the maturity of the notes required (usually 1, 2, 3 or 6 months); and (iii) the issue date. Telex normally to be received by 11.00 am. B. Promptly upon receipt of the telex from the issuer the tender agent sends a telex to the tender panel members notifying them of the amount, issue date and maturity requested and inviting tenders for the euronotes.

Issue date minus 3 days:

A. If the tender agent wishes to submit a tender it must do so by 10.00 am directly to the issuer (ie before it has the benefit of seeing the other members' bids).

B. By noon the tender agent must have received all tenders from tender panel members expressed by reference to LIBOR (eg LIBOR plus 0.05% pa or LIBOR less 0.02% pa).

C. By 1.00 pm the tender agent notifies the issuer of all tenders received, giving details of amounts and yields as well as the names of tenderers.

D. By 3.00 pm the issuer instructs the tender agent to accept certain tenders in accordance with the terms of the tender panel agreement.

E. Underwriting banks are notified whether they will be called upon to purchase unsold notes.

Issue date minus 2 days:

A. By 9.00 am the tender agent notifies the tender panel members whether their tenders have been accepted or not.

B. The relevant LIBOR is set around 11.00 am by two or three reference banks. (The issuing agent can also act as reference agent for this purpose.)

C. By noon tender panel members whose tenders were accepted are notified of the issue price (ie a US dollar amount) to be paid to the issuer.

Issue date:

A. The issuing agent authenticates the euronotes.

B. The issuing agent delivers the euronotes to or to the order of each successful tender panel member.

C. The tender panel members transfer by 10.00 am (New York time) the issue price into the issuer's New York bank account. The tender agent or the issuing agent may act as collecting bank for this purpose.

Some tender panels shortened the period between issue request and issue date to four days. Early facilities tended to have quite long periods, often as much as ten days.

TENDER PANEL VARIATIONS

There were, as time went on, some variations on the basic tender panel structure described above. We see in Table 6 that the tender agent, if it wishes to make a bid, must do so prior to other tender panel members making theirs. This is so that it may not learn privileged information from the other bids in order to better make its own. In some facilities, for example, Associates Corporation of North America's £250m euronote issuance facility signed in June 1985, the tender agent actually notified tender panel members of its own bid when it sent them the invitation to tender. One of the rights the tender agent was allowed in this facility was to purchase euronotes (after the initial tender) up to 20% of the tranche offered at a yield equal to the average yield that would have been achieved by the issuer if it had accepted tenders in such a way as to obtain the lowest yield on those euronotes. If the tender agent had bid for less than 20% of the euronotes being offered then it could only exercise its right to purchase euronotes after the initial tender up to the percentage for which it did tender.

Using the bidding pattern in Example 3 above and assuming that the tender agent is Bank L, an example of this option can be provided as follows:

Example 4

Tender agent's notified bid: $14,000,000 LIBOR plus 0.125% pa
Percentage of issue request: 23.3%

Therefore, Bank L has the right to purchase up to 20% of the offered tranche, that is $12,000,000 at the lowest average yield that would have been accepted for this amount in the tender.

To award the $12,000,000 at the lowest average yield, we have to take the lowest bids of Banks D, A, I, B and C in their entirety which total $11,000,000 and only $1,000,000 of Bank G's lowest bid. This produces an average yield of LIBOR plus 0.005% pa.

Having obtained $12,000,000 of euronotes at that yield, Bank L, as tender agent, advises the following banks that their otherwise accepted bids are not awarded;

Bank D	$1,500,000	@	LIBOR plus 0.07% pa
Bank G	$2,500,000	@	LIBOR plus 0.07% pa
Bank H	$5,000,000	@	LIBOR plus 0.0625% pa

Bank M's $5,000,000 otherwise accepted bid is reduced to $2,000,000. In effect, the cut-off point for accepted bids is lowered.

As the tender agent's bid was advised to other members, it could serve to point members towards the average yield that was expected for that tranche of euronotes. This, of course, depended on the quality of the tender agent and its ability to read the market. Probably more important was the desire of the tender agent (usually the arranger of the facility) to get hold of paper and this enabled it to do so at a known yield provided, however, it had originally bid in the initial tender.

Tender panel agreements also began to provide issuers with the additional flexibility of being able to accept or reject bids received in the tender irrespective of the amount prescribed in the original issue request. In Example 3 therefore the issuer could have accepted all the bids (ie the entire $100 million) if it had found the cost attractive. Alternatively, if it did not like yields above, say, LIBOR plus 0.03% pa,it could have accepted only those bids up to and including Bank I's bid of $8 million, ie a total of $27 million.

Table 7

Typical timetable for absolute rate bidding on a tender panel

Issue date minus 3 days:
  A. Issuer sends a telex to the tender agent requesting an issue of euronotes, specifying:
    (i) the US dollar amount required;
    (ii) the maturity of the notes; and
    (iii) the issue date.
    Telex normally to be received by 11.00 am.
  B. The tender agent, promptly upon receipt of the telex from the issuer, sends a telex to the tender panel members notifying of request details and requesting tenders.

Issue date minus 2 days:
  A. The tender agent, if it wishes to submit a bid, must do so by 10.00 am directly to the issuer. The bid must be a money-market yield unrelated to any benchmark.
  B. Tender panel members must submit their bids by 10.30 am to the tender agent.
  C. The tender agent notifies the issuer of the bids, usually by 11.00–11.30 am.
  D. The issuer will have 30 minutes to decide which bids to accept and therefore will notify the tender agent by 11.30 am or 12.00 noon.
  E. The tender agent notifies tender panel members whether their bids have been accepted or not.
  F. By mid-afternoon (3.00–3.30 pm) successful tender panel members are notified of the issue price (ie a US dollar amount) to be paid to the issuer.

Issue date:
  A. The issuing agent authenticates the euronotes.
  B. The issuing agent delivers the euronotes to or to the order of each successful tender panel member.
  C. The tender panel members transfer by 10.00 am (New York time) the issue price into the issuer's New York bank account.

The market tended to move into two camps, those favouring sole placing agency and those upholding the tender panel as the fairest and most effective distribution method. Whilst the pros and cons of these two methods are analysed in chapter 4 below, it should be said here that issuers began to favour the tender panel because it allowed them to raise cheaper funds through the auction method rather than having euronotes purchased by the sole placing agent at the cap rate. Underwriting banks also complained that sole placing agency did not allow them to share in the earnings derived from the placement of euronotes. It became clear that sole placing agency had to adapt without compromising its exponents' ideals of control of price, performance accountability and orderly distribution of paper.

ISSUER SET MARGIN (ISM)

It was Merrill Lynch Capital Markets which, having innovated the sole placing agency revolving underwriting facility, now provided that crucial adaptation. It responded to the need for the price of the euronote to be determined by the investor market rather than the credit back-stop. It also responded to the need to include underwriting banks in the distribution of euronotes. The new technique was called the 'Issuer Set Margin' (ISM).

The technique is what the name suggests: the issuer itself selects the margin above LIBOR which will apply to the euronotes in a particular offering. As with any euronote issuance facility there is a maximum margin above which euronotes cannot be sold and the issuer may set its margin at any level equal to or below that maximum margin. Unlike the sole placing agency a group of underwriters is selected to form a 'placing group' to which these ISM euronotes are offered first. The issuer usually consults with some of the placing group members as well as the principal placing agent in order to determine what the market considers the correct margin for the euronotes being offered. Normally, placing group members are senior underwriters with the largest commitments in the facility; sometimes all the underwriters belong to the placing group. Each placing group member can elect to purchase at the ISM usually up to 50% of its pro-rata share of any issue of euronotes. Because each placing group member only has a right to purchase euronotes up to a maximum of 50% of its commitment under the facility and because there are other underwriters not in the placing group, the principal placing agent (normally, the bank which alternatively would be the sole placing agent) is therefore always assured a supply of paper.

In the event that some or all of the placing group members do not subscribe euronotes at the ISM the principal placing agent is itself obliged to seek to place their unsold notes at the ISM as well as the amount above each bank's 50% pro-rata share. If the principal placing agent is not able to place the remaining euronotes, then the underwriters are required to purchase the euronotes at the maximum margin.

Table 8

Typical timetable for the issuer set margin procedure

| Issue date minus 5 days: | A. | ISM agent receives by 11.00 a m a request to issue euronotes specifying the US dollar amount, the issue date, maturity and the issuer set margin selected. |
| | B. | ISM agent informs placing group members of the details of the issue request. |

| Issue date minus 4 days: | A. | Each placing group member gives notice to the ISM agent whether it wishes to take up euronotes at the issuer set margin. |
| | B. | The ISM agent informs the issuer of the amounts taken up by placing group members at the issuer set margin. |

| Issue date minus 3 days: | A. | The principal placing agent informs the issuer of the amount of euronotes it is willing to place. |
| | B. | The principal placing agent will inform the underwriters of the amounts of euronotes, if any, they are required to purchase pursuant to their underwriting commitments. |

| Issue date minus 2 days: | A. | The relevant LIBOR is set around 11.00 a m by two or three reference banks. (The issuing agent may act as reference agent for this purpose.) |
| | B. | Placing group members who have elected to take up euronotes are informed of the issue price payable to the issuer. (Likewise the principal placing agent, but it usually fulfils this function itself.) |

| Issue date: | A. | The issuing agent authenticates the euronotes. |
| | B. | The issuing agent delivers the euronotes to the order of the placing group members and the principal placing agent against payment by them of the issue price into the issuer's New York bank account. |

Any euronotes subscribed by underwriters in the placing group at the ISM are deducted from their individual commitments so that upon allocation of unsold euronotes, no underwriter would be obliged to purchase euronotes which would bring its total to more than its commitment in the facility. Let us illustrate this with an example.

Example 5

Issuer:	ISM Corporation
Facility amount:	$100 million
Underwriting banks:	5 banks at $20 million each
Placing group:	All underwriting banks have the right to purchase euronotes up to 50% of their pro-rata commitment
Maximum margin (cap rate):	LIBOR plus 0.125% p a
Issue amount:	$40 million
Issuer set margin selected:	LIBOR plus 0.05% p a

The issue amount of $40 million means that the placing group members are each permitted to subscribe up to $4 million of euronotes at the issuer set margin of LIBOR plus 0.05% p a.

If the banks elect to subscribe as follows:

Bank 1	$1,000,000
Bank 2	$1,000,000
Bank 3	nil
Bank 4	$2,000,000 ·
Bank 5	nil
Total subscribed:	$4,000,000

The principal placing agent will thus be required to seek to place $36 million ($40 million less $4 million) on its own.

Should the principal placing agent be unable to place any of the euronotes, then the remaining $36 million will have to be purchased at the cap rate by the underwriters pro-rata to their underwriting commitments, subtracting any notes already purchased at the ISM.

Therefore, the allocations are made as follows:

Bank 1	$7,000,000	($8,000,000–$1,000,000)
Bank 2	$7,000,000	($8,000,000–$1,000,000)
Bank 3	$8,000,000	($8,000,000–nil)
Bank 4	$6,000,000	($8,000,000–$2,000,000)
Bank 5	$8,000,000	($8,000,000–nil)
	$36,000,000	

The issuer's average cost for the offered tranche is LIBOR plus 0.1175% p a (ie $4 million at LIBOR + 0.05% p a and $36 million at LIBOR + 0.125% p a).

In the above example the proportion of a bank's commitment in a euronote issuance facility available to it to purchase euronotes at the ISM was 50%. This proportion is not an absolute and considerable flexibility has been shown in establishing this proportion to suit the particular needs of specific transactions. In some cases where the underwriting banks are divided into two groups – often called managing underwriters and co-managing underwriters – only the former might be members of the placing group with the principal placing agent placing euronotes on behalf of the latter. Managing underwriters might be able to purchase up to 100% of their pro-rata commitments in such circumstances. A further refinement exists in multi-tiered syndications (lead managers, co-lead managers and managers) where the lead managers are allowed to purchase up to 100% of their commitments, the co-lead managers 50% and managers zero per cent; any amount of notes not subscribed at the ISM by the co-lead managers are first made available for subscription by the lead managers. Only if the lead managers do not subscribe these notes does the principal placing agent seek to place them. The technique is capable of many nuances and is highly flexible in order to suit particular circumstances.

Whatever structure is selected the principal placing agent's placement skills are critical to the underwriters, since they may well be allocated euronotes in a facility in which they did not expect such allocation. The quality of the principal placing agent will thus be one of the factors in a placing group member's decision to purchase paper at the ISM. For the issuer too the principal placing agent's advice is vital. If the ISM is pitched too low the issuer's cost can rise immediately to the cap rate. By pushing the market too far by one basis point on the ISM, the euronotes may not be bought by investors and the issuer might have to pay interest at the cap rate.

The ISM method is not a compromise of the theoretical principles behind sole placing agency since the issuance of euronotes still occurs in a manner controlled by the issuer and the principal placing agent. It meets an important need of some underwriting banks to be involved in the distribution of the paper but does not impose an 'anonymous' and unwieldy group of banks on the issuer. Co-ordination, responsibility for orderliness of the market and ultimate performance accountability remain largely with the principal placing agent. If the tender panel structure had not prevailed for reasons that had little to do with optimal euronote placement, the ISM structure really deserved to prevail since it had almost all the theoretical and, indeed, practical arguments on its side – this is an area which will be reviewed more fully in the next chapter.

It is estimated that in the sole placing agency and ISM distribution methods probably less than 5% of euronotes issued have been unable to be sold and therefore allocated to underwriting banks.

THE CONTINUOUS TENDER PANEL

If sole placing agency spawned the ISM in an attempt to adapt to syndication pressures and to changes in distribution techniques, then the tender panel spawned the continuous tender panel structure ('CTP') really only to correct the perceived deficiencies of tender panel bidding. It was a piece of innovative thinking in a fast developing market and borrowed conceptually from the long-term bond markets. The structure was the hallmark of its inventor, Dean Witter Capital Markets–International Limited and they used it for the first time on a $100 million facility for Malayan Banking Berhad signed in December 1984. It lies somewhere between the sole placing agency and the tender panel, drawing on the strengths and trying to avoid the weaknesses of both techniques.

The operation of the CTP is relatively straightforward and is co-ordinated by a CTP-manager. When the issuer makes a request of the CTP-manager for an issue of euronotes, the latter informs *all* the facility underwriters by telex. The CTP-manager establishes a selling period for the euronotes being offered (say six or seven days) similar in some ways to a Eurobond issue. The CTP-manager and the underwriters now form a tender panel which operates continuously (hence the nomenclature) until the end of the selling period. The CTP-manager establishes something called the 'strike offering yield' (SOY) being the yield level at which it will sell euronotes to CTP-members who wish to subscribe. CTP members are not obliged to bid for euronotes. The SOY is, in fact, the yield at which the CTP-manager is offering paper to its investors at the same time and, of course, may change in line with market conditions during the selling period. It cannot be above the cap rate contractually agreed in the facility documentation which represents the issuer's maximum cost.

The CTP-manager will satisfy tenders from CTP members at the SOY up to their pro-rata underwriting commitments and any amount thus subscribed is deducted from the underwriter's pro-rata commitment in the event of an allocation of unsold notes. If available, additional euronotes over and above pro-rata commitments may be sold to underwriters. It should be noted that potentially the CTP-manager may not be able to place any paper because each underwriter can take up its entire pro-rata commitment. This is unlikely to happen as the CTP-manager is likely to establish the SOY through consultation with its own investors and it is able to sell euronotes to these investors from the outset. Underwriters, therefore, are only able to obtain euronotes to the extent that they are *available*.

Additional flexibility is given by the CTP-manager in allowing 'protection'. Should the CTP-member wish to sound out its investors and have a secure supply of paper to offer them at a known yield, the CTP-manager will hold the SOY for an agreed period of time to permit such action. Typically the protection period would be about 15 minutes, sufficient time to call the investor with a firm price and obtain its decision. The concept of protection is borrowed from the Eurobond markets.

If, at the end of the selling period, some euronotes remain unsold these are purchased by the underwriters pro-rata to their commitments at the cap rate. Allowance is made for euronotes already purchased by the underwriters in the CTP.

Let us consider an example:

Example 6

Issuer:	CTP Corporation
Facility amount:	$100 million
Underwriting banks:	10 banks, each with $10 million commitment (Bank A through Bank J)
Maximum margin (cap rate):	LIBOR plus 0.125% p a
Issue tranche:	$40 million

The issue tranche is offered by the CTP-manager to the ten underwriting banks as members of the continuous tender panel at an initial SOY of LIBOR plus

0.05% pa. Each bank has, therefore, the right to subscribe $4 million of euronotes (40% of $10 million).

Let us assume that Banks A, B and C are able immediately to subscribe their full pro-rata commitments, ie $4 million each at the SOY on day 1.

Banks D and E are protected by the CTP-manager on day 2 for a period of 15 minutes at the same SOY for $4 million each and during that period Bank D confirms to the CTP-manager a subscription of $2 million and Bank E of zero.

The CTP-manager itself sells $14 million of which $9 million at the original SOY and then a further $5 million at a new SOY established later of LIBOR plus 0.0625% pa. The total amount of euronotes sold is therefore:

Bank A	$4,000,000 @ LIBOR + 0.05% pa
Bank B	$4,000,000 @ LIBOR + 0.05% pa
Bank C	$4,000,000 @ LIBOR + 0.05% pa
Bank D	$2,000,000 @ LIBOR + 0.05% pa
Banks E, F, G, H, I, J	zero
CTP-manager	$9,000,000 @ LIBOR + 0.05% pa
CTP-manager	$5,000,000 @ LIBOR + 0.0625% pa
TOTAL	$28,000,000

Of the initial tranche of $40 million, there remains unsold $12 million of euronotes which are purchased at the cap rate of LIBOR plus 0.125% pa by the underwriters pro-rata to their commitments after deducting euronotes purchased at the SOY. In this example, the $12 million is allocated as to $2 million each to Banks E, F, G, H, I and J.

Calculating the cost to the issuer in the above example depends on the arrangements set out in the documentation of the euronote issuance facility. It is believed that some facilities borrowed a feature of the sole placing agency RUF in that the issuer sold its tranche at the cap rate and the CTP-manager and CTP-members retained any turn arising from sales to investors at below the cap rate. This, of course, solves the problem of allowing underwriting banks to share in the placement of euronotes but retains the basic disadvantage of establishing the cost of euronotes to the issuer at the cost of the credit back-stop not at a market-driven yield. This disadvantage was in large part solved by some facilities establishing a sharing of the cost-savings between issuer and CTP-members.

In the debate between the ISM and tender panel camps one of the main criticisms levelled against the latter is the absence of responsibility for price and of orderly distribution by a single bank. The CTP structure skillfully addresses this problem and largely solves it. The CTP-manager in setting the SOY is responsible for overall pricing of the euronotes. If it keeps the SOY unrealistically low during the selling period – either through misreading the market or through trying to withhold paper from the CTP-members – the underwriters will know because they will be allocated unsold euronotes at the cap rate. If they have already submitted unsuccessful bids to the CTP-manager above the SOY, they will certainly complain in order to ensure there is no recurrence. The CTP structure also offers one of the most important elements of all distribution methods, security of a supply of paper to CTP-members. CTP-members are able to develop an investor base for the issuer's euronotes. In theory the CTP-manager can sell the whole tranche at the SOY before the CTP-members can organise discussions with their investors, but in practice an entire tranche is not sold immediately and CTP-members do obtain paper.

It is claimed that in no CTP facility have any euronotes failed to be sold by the CTP-manager; therefore no allocations of unsold notes have ever been made to underwriting banks.

Table 9

Timetable of an issue of euronotes through the continuous tender panel

Issue date minus 7 days:	A. Issuer sends a telex to the CTP-manager requesting an issue of euronotes, specifying: (i) the US dollar amount required; (ii) the maturity of the notes required; and (iii) the issue date. The telex would normally be received by 11.00 am. B. The CTP-manager sends the details contained in the telex to the underwriting banks. Those underwriting banks permitted to be members of the CTP are invited to form a CTP for this tranche.
Issue date minus 7 days – minus 2 days	A. The CTP is in session during this period, usually up to 10.15 am of issue date minus 2 days. B. The CTP-manager establishes a SOY at which CTP-members may purchase euronotes. C. During this period the SOY may be changed to reflect market conditions. D. The CTP-manager can during this period offer 'protection' to CTP-members.
Issue date minus 2 days:	A. The CTP-manager confirms to the issuer the amounts of euronotes purchased and the yield(s) at which they are purchased. It further confirms to the issuer and underwriting banks whether any unsold euronotes are to be purchased by underwriting banks. B. The CTP selling period terminates at 10.15 am. C. The relevant LIBOR is set around 11.00 am by two or three reference banks. (The issuing agent can also act as reference agent for this purpose.)

	D.	The CTP-members and, if applicable, the underwriting banks are notified of the issue price (ie a US dollar amount) to be paid to the issuer.
Issue date:	A.	The issuing agent authenticates the euronotes.
	B.	The issuing agent delivers the euronotes to the order of the purchasing CTP-members and/or the underwriting banks.
	C.	The CTP-members and/or the underwriting banks transfer by 10.00 am (New York time) the issue price into the issuer's New York bank account.

GLOSSARY

Although it is not within the scope of this book to review the details of various euronote issuance facility structures which lie more in the field of syndication than note placement, it is useful to explain some of the acronyms which are used to identify these facilities.

(i) RUF: Revolving underwriting facility

A term first used by Merrill Lynch International Limited denoting a facility which used the sole placing agency distribution method. Strictly speaking, the RUF should denote exclusively this structure but has now become associated by many as the generic term for euronote issuance facilities.

(ii) NIF: Note issuance facility

It is difficult to determine when this term was first used but, like 'RUF', has become for many the generic term for all manner of euronote issuance facilities irrespective of distribution method. It refers in its accepted sense to a facility using the tender panel distribution method.

(iii) SNIF: Standby note issuance facility

First used by Chase Manhattan Limited, it is identical in structure to a NIF but emphasises that the facility is intended not to be drawn but to act as a back-stop to other sources of funding.

(iv) TRUF: Transferable revolving underwriting facility

Another term invented by Merrill Lynch which denotes a RUF in which the underwriting commitment of a participant bank can be easily transferred to another bank. The transferability should not be confused with negotiability and it is effected by a form of words which makes the transfer process more convenient to execute.

(v) BONUS: Borrower's option for notes and underwritten standby

This term was invented by Bank of America International Limited to describe a facility in which there is a maximum amount underwritten by banks but where also the amount of euronotes permitted to be issued under the facility is higher than that underwritten amount. The first BONUS was a $300 million facility arranged in February 1985 for AB Volvo and comprised a $150 million committed standby and $150 million uncommitted note placement facility. Banks are obliged to lend funds under the committed standby but not in the uncommitted facility.

(vi) MOF: Multiple option facility

Also called a multiple facility, the MOF is in essence a revolving credit underwritten by banks which offers the borrower various other borrowing options, of which euronotes may only be one. Such options might also include multicurrency loan advances, US$ bankers' acceptances or sterling acceptances, all of which are usually offered through uncommitted tender panels where members are expected, but not obliged, to bid. The facility is designed to offer the borrower as much flexibility as possible in the options provided.

CHAPTER 4

The euronote explosion

In explaining and analysing the evolution of the euronote and the various attempts to establish a Euro-commercial paper market the previous chapters have described a number of stimuli and trends prevailing in the financial markets during the period from the early 1970s to the end of 1983. It is now clear how these stimuli and trends over the following two years to 1985 brought about that crucial step from the euronote issued pursuant to an underwritten credit facility to the note issued under a non-underwritten Euro-commercial paper programme. We will now examine the continuation of the market's evolution in 1984. Tables 10 and 11 serve to develop further the statistical picture initially presented in Tables 1 and 2 above.

Table 10

Euronote issuance facilities

VOLUME AND NUMBER OF TRANSACTIONS (1978–86)

Year	Volume ($m)	Number of transactions
1978–83	8,862	84
1984	17,120	83
1985	39,950	235
1986 (est)	23,109	137

Source: Euromoney

1984 saw an explosion in the use of the euronote issuance facility with over $17 billion of facilities arranged and with as many transactions in that year as in the previous six years together. 1985 experienced an even bigger explosion with almost $40 billion of facilities arranged comprising an astonishing 235 individual transactions – about one per business day. The average facility size doubled from just over $100 million up to 1983 to $206m in 1984, but fell back to $170 million in 1985. The 1984 figure is somewhat distorted by four facilities of $1 billion or more arranged in that year: Kingdom of Sweden ($4 billion), New Zealand ($1.5 billion), Kingdom of Denmark ($1 billion) and Nestlé Holdings Inc ($1 billion).

Table 11 breaks out these volume figures by type of borrower and reveals that a sea-change was taking place. Previous analysis showed how bank and sovereign issuers had come to dominate the market with 84% of transaction volume in 1983. The following year saw this percentage drop to 58% and in 1985 to 26% although the average volume remained fairly constant. From a

Table 11

Euronote issuance facilities

VOLUME ($M) AND NUMBER OF TRANSACTIONS BY TYPE OF BORROWER (1978–86)

	1978–83	1984	1985	1986
		($m)		
Sovereign	1750 (6)	7225 (6)	3035 (7)	8868 (25)
Supranational	250 (3)	500 (2)	850 (2)	200 (1)
Corporate	2119 (22)	6676 (43)	28769 (157)	9132 (60)
Bank	4743 (53)	2719 (32)	7296 (69)	4909 (51)
Total	8862 (84)	17120 (83)	39950 (235)	23109 (137)

Source: Euromoney

small but growing base up to 1983 corporate issuers became in 1984 the second largest issuer by volume ($6,676 million) and by far the largest in number of transactions (43). On both counts in 1985 they became the overwhelmingly dominant issuer group with 72% of market volume ($28.769 million) and 67% of the number of transactions (157). The corporate borrower had finally made its mark.

It has been suggested that the slowness of corporate borrowers to recognise and use the euronote issuance facility as a core borrowing medium owes much to traditional conservatism and the irregularity of corporate medium-term funding needs. Possibly they had been waiting for the product to become legitimised through increased usage and to prove itself viable in the market. It is open to debate whether the 1984 explosion was a result of a sudden collective recognition by corporates that the euronote issuance facility was a legitimate borrowing structure giving access to a large investor base ready and waiting to buy their euronotes. This presupposes that euronotes *would* be issued under these facilities and that the whole point of them was to enable the borrower's euronotes to be purchased by a wide range of investors, thereby diversifying the borrower's sources of funds. This quite clearly was not the case. In most instances euronotes were *not* being issued because the facilities were simply being used as a cheap back-stop for borrowings from other sources such as the domestic commercial paper market. Cheap is the operative word – the chief objective of most issuers in establishing a euronote issuance facility was to effect a low standby cost. Their initial aim was not to issue euronotes since few believed them to be a cheaper source of borrowings. The key trend of the continuing decline in credit pricing, inextricably linked with the equally key trend of a fiercely competitive banking environment, had created a curious phenomenon – banks on the one hand were creating complicated structures for the issuance of euronotes and holding out to issuers the prospect of cheaper borrowings; issuers on the other hand were focussing more on the undrawn cost of the facilities, regarding the issuance of euronotes of secondary importance and generally doubtful of their cost-effectiveness. In negotiations borrowers concentrated more on the underwriting fee than on the margin above LIBOR. The vague promise of issuing euronotes for many, therefore, was the cover for obtaining a cheap standby facility.

With over 400 foreign banks operating in London since 1980 (470 in 1984) there was bound to be competition. With the disintermediation process continuing apace – due mainly to the securitisation of commercial banking products – there was even more intense competition. Not only were there many banks willing to join euronote issuance facility syndicates as a means of achieving their objective of increasing their international loan portfolios, there was also a smaller (but considerable) number of the larger banks extremely keen to compensate for the erosion by euronote issuance facilities of their traditional lending business by seeking to arrange these facilities and to develop their euronote placement capabilities. An important driving-force became the banks' league-table positions for arranging such facilities and their reputation as a placer of paper.

It is impossible to convey in writing the intensity of competition during what must have been two of the most extraordinary years in recent banking history. Bankers had never made so many proposals to their customers and some were sending them to borrowers they had never even met. Borrowers, especially the largest and most creditworthy, might have had as many as 30 proposals on their desks from banks wishing to arrange for them a euronote issuance facility. Many borrowers confessed bewilderment at the frenetic activity of banks and confusion about the various structures, acronyms and distribution methods being proposed. Different names and the alteration of minor elements were claimed as major innovations but, on the whole, the basic facility structures remained the same. However, one thing was clear – mandates were being sought not only on the benefits of certain facility structures and distribution techniques, but also on *price*.

The 1984 explosion can be attributed in no small measure to all borrower types, and especially corporates, yielding to the temptation of cheap financing. Even when a borrowing need was not expected, few borrowers could resist a facility, however small, to refinance an existing standby. Pricing levels had never been so low. A few examples of this trend of declining pricing are convincing. New Zealand, which agreed a commitment fee of 0.25% p a on its $500 million note purchase facility in 1981, increased the facility to $750 million in 1982 on which it paid 0.1875% p a on the first $250 million and 0.25% p a on the remainder. Two years later it doubled the size of the facility to $1.5 billion and agreed a facility fee of 0.10% p a. The Kingdom of Sweden raised in September 1984 the largest ever facility of this type (actually a multiple facility) at $4 billion on which the facility fee was 0.125% p a. One year later it renegotiated the facility reducing the amount to $2 billion and the facility fee to 0.05% p a for the first five years and 0.0625% p a for the remaining five years. OECD figures confirm the trend, revealing that international bank loan margins on average had almost halved in 1985 compared to their 1983 levels.[1]

It was the Kingdom of Denmark's $1 billion facility which prefaced new levels of pricing. Signed in July 1984 the facility fee was a mere 0.05% p a. For such a prime borrower the syndication met unprecedented difficulties and a boycott by certain major banks trying to stem the tide of falling credit pricing.

1 *Financial Market Trends*, October 1985.

The syndication was still successful and proved emphatically that it was a borrower's market. Henceforth highly-rated borrowers came to the market with facility fees of around 0.05–0.0625% pa. Nestlé Holdings Inc's facility even had an element of 0.03125% pa in the facility fee. Lower quality borrowers also began to achieve rates below 0.10% pa. At the time of writing some single-A rated borrowers are capable of obtaining facility fees of 0.0625% pa, unprecedented low levels in the Euromarkets.

It is worth mentioning here that despite their cheap pricing the facilities incurred much higher arrangement expenses for borrowers. Documentation for a euronote issuance facility, and especially for a multiple facility, was longer and more complex than for a normal revolving credit because of the operational mechanics required for issuing notes. US legal issues were complicated and confusing, requiring detailed selling restrictions. Legal expenses were consequently higher and the issuer was required to pay not only facility agency expenses but those too of the tender agent. In some cases total expenses were double those of a normal revolving credit, but the overall cost benefits of the standby pricing usually outweighed the incidental expenses and inconvenience of negotiating the facility.

SOLE PLACING AGENCY VERSUS TENDER PANEL

The fierce competition for mandates had its echo in the rivalry between banks believing in the merits of one euronote distribution method over another. Opinions were tenaciously held as to the technical supremacy of the sole placing agency whilst a powerful camp supported the tender panel.

For the issuer the tender panel could boast a critical advantage over its rival structure, the sole placing agency. It was the method which priced the euronote, and hence the issuer's borrowing cost, in line with the market for that paper. Contrast this with the sole placing agency method which still tied the price of the euronote to the cost of the credit back-stop. The difference between the cap rate and the accepted bids from the tender panel members accrues to the issuer; in the sole placing agency, unless there is an arrangement to the contrary, the placing agent keeps any difference between the cap rate and the yield at which it sells the euronotes. Because issuers gain the benefit of the differential between the cap rate and accepted bids, there is obvious issuer support for the tender panel method. The sole placing agency suffered because of this. Fewer major borrowers began to use sole placing agency and the method was amended by the introduction of the issuer set margin which allowed the issuer to issue at below the cap rate.

Critics of the tender panel contend that no one bank in a tender panel has any explicit commitment to developing an investor base for the issuer's euronotes, whereas a sole placing agent is entirely and individually responsible for this development. Indeed, the sole placing agent is 'exposed' in good and bad markets alike and cannot conceal his performance from the issuer. In theory, this criticism ought not to be true since the issuer has the information to judge the performance in a tender panel of all the banks which, having become members of their own volition, should be aiming to support each tranche of euronotes. In practice, however, the criticism is largely true for reasons that have to do with the actual practical behaviour of tender panel members rather than with any theoretical assumptions.

The manner in which the tender panel was constituted and structured led to certain behaviour patterns. In the first place, during the syndication process banks would make it a condition of their accepting an underwriting commitment that they also became a member of the tender panel. This precondition was set irrespective of whether banks were skilled in euronote placement or not. In some cases membership was quite logical and advisable especially where banks had respectable euronote placement capabilities. In others it was less obvious but, since some banks claimed that these capabilities were being built and tender panel membership assisted the building process, they were included. It has since turned out that not every bank successfully built such capabilities. There were occasions when banks joined the tender panel even when they had no intention of developing placement capabilities, simply because every other bank was invited to join and exclusion was less easy to accept than inclusion. Some thought that there would be significant additional income to be derived from placing an issuer's euronotes. It became a matter of corporate pride to be included as a tender panel member with exclusion considered a sleight. No arranger dared therefore to risk unsuccessful syndication by not inviting underwriters to join the tender panel so that they might also share in the earnings derived from euronote placement. In most syndications, as a matter of course, the lead manager would stipulate in the invitation telex to prospective participant banks that they would automatically be members of the tender panel. In short, little care was taken to ensure that banks had the requisite skills for the placement task being asked of them. Additional banks which were not underwriting banks but recognised as skilled in euronote placement were invited into the tender panel in order to strengthen its overall placement power.

Because of the wide diversity of banks in tender panels there was naturally a wide divergence of bidding for euronotes. In the early tenders under a facility banks typically would bid aggressively for euronotes, often because they felt they were impressing the issuer. Such was their aggression that the yield bid could be so low that it was afterwards impossible to place the euronotes with investors. Thus they became on the bidder's books a very cheap loan to the issuer or, as frequently occurred, they were 'dumped' into the market as a loss-cutting exercise. The defenders of sole placing agency were reinforced in their view that this behaviour only resulted in erratic yield levels, helping neither issuer nor investor. A sole placing agent could not permit himself such aggression. Paper flooding the market at distress yields could only have come from one source. Its duty was to establish a competitive but consistent yield level and maintain an orderly market.

After the early flush of enthusiasm tender panel members tended to settle into a pattern and often, though with exceptions, only a small number of banks began to win paper regularly. In small tender panels this might be only one or two banks but as many as eight or ten in the larger ones. During the selling period investors might be contacted by a number of members of the same tender panel and they would often play one bank off against the other. As they were not assured a supply of paper on the tender panel each would bid at ever lower yields to obtain paper and satisfy the same investor. Obviously all this was avoided with the sole placing agency method. Because of the erratic performance of tender panel members even the claim that it ensured wider distribution of an issuer's paper became less persuasive.

The sole placing agency camp also claimed that an underwriting bank which, usually through its investment banking subsidiary, was also a member of the tender panel was faced with a conflict of interest. Why should one bid at below the cap rate for euronotes which it might not be possible to sell, when, if insufficient euronotes were bid for overall, the other would obtain an allocation of euronotes at that cap rate in any case. This argues for unaggressive and insufficient bidding and this may explain the behaviour of those banks who regularly bid close to the maximum margin or who did not bid at all. The general experience, however, was quite the reverse with, as we mentioned above, aggressive bidding becoming the norm.

The argument that the uncertainty of supply on the tender panel was not conducive to the development of a consistent and stable investor base was, like several arguments put forward by the sole placing agency camp, valid. Although the same group of banks began consistently to win paper, the auction process ensured that they were never certain to do so. Even though a bank may have pitched its bid at the right theoretical level for an issuer's paper, a mistaken bid or a tender panel member deciding to show periodic support could mean that bank losing the paper and having to miss an investor sale. Though most banks in the market would admit this weakness of the tender panel method, aggressive bidding meant lower borrowing costs for issuers and issuers' influence remained the overriding determining factor in the markets.

Perversely, therefore, the arguments for and against these two distribution methods were motivated as much by the concern about wide distribution and constant issuing yields as by syndication considerations. Since banks in sole placing agency facilities could not participate in the placement of euronotes and since many banks, rightly or wrongly, sought to develop their activities in this field, it became quite simply harder for sole placing agency revolving underwriting facilities to be syndicated, especially those for major borrowers. In mid-1984 the terms of a $500 million facility for the Kingdom of Spain had to be changed in mid-syndication because of the resistance of banks ostensibly to the sole placing agency feature. Changes were forced upon the lead manager which finally permitted underwriting banks with a certain level of participation to place euronotes up to 50% of their commitment. This was really the first large facility for a major borrower to experience syndication difficulties at this time though the $1 billion Kingdom of Denmark also suffered a small boycott but was syndicated without any change of terms. Whilst most banks used the argument of not liking the euronote distribution method for declining to participate in the Kingdom of Spain transaction, the prime motive is thought to have been the desire of banks to take a stance on deteriorating pricing levels.

We reviewed previously the theoretical problems regarding performance and accountability but in operational terms the tender panel can be quite inflexible. Typical constraints in the mechanics of the tender panel are:

– there is usually a prescribed maximum and minimum amount of euronotes to be offered in any tranche, e g a minimum of $25 million and a maximum of $50 million to be issued at any one time

- tranches have to be issued in multiples of $5 million
- tranches can only be issued at minimum intervals of, say, ten business days
- tranches are stipulated to be in even month maturities, usually 30, 60, 90, 180 days; no broken period maturities are permitted
- usually one tranche of a single maturity can be issued at one time.

If you add to these general constraints the fact that the issuer has to notify the tender agent of an issue request between five and ten days prior to the date he requires receipt of funds, it becomes clear that the tender panel is cumbersome and poorly designed to capitalise on market opportunities as they arise. With so many borrowers using their euronote issuance facilities as standbys this may hardly have mattered. Indeed, with so many facilities being arranged and so little experience of paper being issued into the market, the operational details of the tender panel were often hastily decided and without much first-hand knowledge of investor requirements. In several instances issuers renegotiated the operational details shortly after establishing the facility because the first few issues showed up the inefficiencies of the original structure. Two of the principle amendments were (i) to shorten the period between issue request and receipt of funds to as little as possible, with four or five days becoming the norm, and (ii) to introduce absolute rate bidding rather than LIBOR-related bidding. Because of their necessarily organised structure distribution techniques under committed facilities proliferate LIBOR-related bidding. With the time required to collect bids and award them, bids have to be tied to a benchmark that moves in line with short-term interest rates. The only absolute element of the bid is the margin above or below LIBOR. Absolute rate bidding requires banks normally to leave a bid with the tender agent and issuer for up to two hours which in itself is too long in a market where interest rates can move sharply in either direction. As a result absolute rate bidding is only infrequently used. These structural amendments enable the issuer to shorten the period between issue request and receipt of funds to three days, comprising one day for organising the issue request and bids and two days for issuing the euronotes and arranging settlement. Absolute rate bidding does not obviate the need for those two days after bid acceptance.

In the end more transactions were arranged on a tender panel basis not least because this offered the issuer a potentially cheaper cost since any benefit of a yield bid lower than the cap rate accrued directly to it. The sole placing agency fell away to be replaced by the ISM structure which allowed issuers to share in the benefit of selling euronotes below the cap rate. However, this came really too late to prevent the tender panel structure from establishing itself as the main distribution method for major borrowers and ISM became increasingly used for smaller less well-known borrowers which benefitted greatly from the sponsorship and guidance of a skilled principal placing agent.

The tender panel method dominated the market also because of its appeal to prospective underwriters who could share in any placment commissions and because it made syndication easier. Without it the larger borrowers could not have syndicated their facilities.

EURONOTE ISSUANCE AND INVESTORS

Having analysed distribution methods and reviewed both the competitive and pricing pressures existing in the marketplace, we should now turn our attention to the actual performance of these methods and what was after all the theoretical 'raison d'être' of euronote issuance facilities – the issuance of euronotes. Clearly not all facilities were used as standbys. Euronotes had been in issue since the earliest facilities such as New Zealand's and investor groups like commercial banks and large insurance companies had been the main purchasers. Distribution structures which priced the euronote at the price of the back-stop generally meant that investors could purchase euronotes at a positive margin over LIBOR. As commercial banks tended to use LIBOR as a benchmark for their marginal cost of funds, then a euronote at a margin above LIBOR became an attractive short-term asset which could be match funded. This is one of the main reasons why commercial banks in the early days were the principle investor group. It also goes some way to explaining why issuers were often dubious about the scope and variety of the investor market and their reluctance to issue paper. Some argued that having their paper sold to commercial banks would be tantamount to using up existing lines of credit and would, in fact, add nothing to their finance sources.

Nevertheless, it has been estimated that $500m–$1 billon of euronotes were outstanding by the end of 1983, between 6% and 11% of total facilities arranged. By the end of 1984 the consensus view was that between $3–5 billion of euronotes were in issue, maintaining the 11% proportion of total facilities arranged. It was in 1984 that outstandings started to rise sharply in absolute terms as high quality borrowers began to use the tender panel method in their facilities, such as Kingdom of Sweden, State Electricity Commission of Victoria, State Electricity Commission of Queensland and Britoil plc. Most of the activity came towards the end of 1984 and, what was the most crucial development in the whole short-term note market, the investor base began to increase and diversify both in volume and type.

In chapter 2 above we described the crisis surrounding international, principally US, banks at the time of the Latin American debt crisis and the Continental Illinois restructuring. The uncertainty about large, money-centre banks caused doubts not only in the minds of smaller and medium-sized banks which possibly established euronote issuance facilities as a defensive funding measure but also, much more importantly, in investors' minds. Suffice it to say that another key trend was establishing itself: investors began to diversify their investment portfolios away from commercial bank risk into corporate and sovereign risk. The simple act of making a time-deposit with a bank or buying its CDs could no longer be executed with the same degree of assurance as before. It was at this time that the corporate investor seriously entered the market. Hitherto almost exclusively wedded to bank-risk instruments, its conservative nature led it into the corporate and sovereign euronote sector principally as a risk-diversification exercise. The attractions of potentially higher-yielding investments were also evident to it. It certainly did not become the largest investor group but in previous attempts at establishing a Euro-commercial paper market the corporate investor had not been a factor and at this juncture this was an important breakthrough for the new market.

It did not take long for major borrowers to realise that they were often a better credit risk and more highly-rated than the underwriting banks 'supporting' them in their euronote issuance facility. Logic suggested that if investors were increasingly prepared to buy paper issued by corporates and sovereigns then they should do so at rates below the deposit and CD rates posted by most commercial banks. The market moved from the relatively comfortable position of selling paper at rates above those at which banks wished to price their assets (LIBOR being taken as this benchmark) to selling paper at below LIBOR and even below LIBID. This level automatically excluded the bank investor which previously bought paper at above-LIBOR levels and placed the asset on the commercial loan book. In order to sustain a real euronote market at these yields it became obvious that a non-bank investor base needed to be developed. Paper that was priced above LIBID but below LIBOR still could not be effectively sold to banks whose benchmark cost of funds was LIBOR. However, investors could be persuaded to buy this paper on the basis that the underlying credit was good and that the yield represented a small but material increase above time-deposits and CDs at LIBID. A large amount of placement business began to be executed on this basis, offering yield improvements for investors and, in some cases offering issuers their first ever borrowing below LIBOR outside of the swap markets.

For the very highly-rated borrowers the question was whether investors really would sacrifice yield for improved investment quality. That is, would investors be prepared to reduce their deposits with international banks and place them in sovereign and corporate euronotes below LIBID? There was much discussion in the market whether this could happen and, when it actually did happen, whether it could sustain itself.[2]

When investment diversification was combined with the fierce competition on tender panels, it came as no surprise that some impressive cost levels began to be achieved by major borrowers. Tables 12 and 13 provide details of the bidding results on the tender panels for the Kingdom of Sweden and Britoil plc,

---

2 Measuring market yields against a LIBID or LIBOR benchmark is common in the euronote and Euro-commercial paper market but can at times be confusing and erroneous. The market definition of LIBID is the interest rate bid by prime banks in order to attract deposits from other prime banks. Yet LIBID can vary between banks reflecting differing perceptions of creditworthiness and differing needs for funds in certain maturities. It is a rate, after all, which can move up or down significantly when markets are unsettled. What is not clear is whether the rate quoted on a bank's electronic screens in the interbank market is the rate quoted to the customer to attact its deposit. In many instances investors are without access to such screens and may find it difficult to verify what exactly LIBID is. At a time when investors were redirecting their funds away from the 'doubtful' banks to those considered of high quality and secure, demand was such that high quality banks were able to reduce their deposit rates for non-bank customers below interbank rates. There is a dichotomy in that euronote distribution techniques such as tender panels demand the use of the LIBID/LIBOR benchmark because banks require it but upon award of paper a bank owns an asset at an absolute yield and will quote that to potential investors. What is clear is that investors do not use LIBID very much as an investment benchmark but rather, each time an investment is to be made, they will compare *absolute yields* on alternative investment instruments. The rate quoted is therefore paramount, not whether it is more, equal to or less than that quoted on a bank's electronic screen in the interbank market. The use of the LIBID/LIBOR benchmark is much more a convenience for banks when referring to their claimed marginal cost of funds and to the required bank yield of their risk assets; it is used extensively in this book in that context.

both very highly rated issuers. The Kingdom of Sweden from its first issue in November 1984 became a benchmark in the market. It is a very good example of bidding patterns in the euronote market.

The first issue of $200 million of three-month paper attracted bids totalling a staggering $1,823 million. The aggression of tender panel members and their enthusiasm in wanting to impress the borrower produced a lowest bid of 0.35% pa below LIBID and the last accepted bid of 0.135% pa below LIBID gave a truly astonishing average of 0.148% pa below LIBID. Eighteen days later a $300 million tender attracted $1,599 million of bids with a lowest bid of 0.17% pa below LIBID and an average of 0.113% pa below LIBID. The tender panel then settled down throughout 1985 and 1986 to a fairly consistent weighted average cost of between 0.07–0.04% pa below LIBID. Up to July 1986 $5.8 billion of euronotes had been raised via the tender panel method.

Similarly, Britoil up to June 1986 had made 34 issues of euronotes under its tender panel with not too dissimilar results. It has a smaller tender panel than the Kingdom of Sweden's (14 banks versus over 40 banks) and comprises mainly close relationship banks. This may explain why less divergence and extremes of bidding were apparent. Britoil's best bid has been 0.083% pa below LIBID and its weighted average accepted bid has been particularly consistent at 0.046% pa below LIBID. In total Britoil raised $815 million from the tender panel method generally through individual tranches of $25 million.

The Kingdom of Sweden and Britoil plc are examples of two of the most professionally handled and successful tender panels. The reason for this was that they both kept a reasonable amount outstanding in the market and generally sought to 'rollover' maturing tranches. Indeed, at one stage the Kingdom of Sweden had $1.1 billion of euronotes outstanding and it became the most liquid issue in the market. However, this is not to say that all of the $1.1 billion was firmly placed with end-investors. Whilst certainly the rapid build-up of outstandings under the facility reflected enormously increased investor interest in such paper, it is fair to say that supply probably outstripped demand. This suggests that tender panel members were holding some paper on their books and we ought now to look at how and why this was the case.

One other aspect of the market appropriate to mention here is that once euronote issuance facilities had run for a year or more some issuers would review the bidding performance of tender panel members. In the case of poor performance such banks might be replaced by those stronger in placement or the tender panel left at a reduced size. Whilst the composition of all tender panels could in theory be changed, issuers probably eschewed such changes if it meant confrontation with relationship banks. On the whole, provided a core of banks wins paper regularly at competitive yields, issuers have opted not to change tender panel composition.

TRADING VERSUS PLACEMENT

If the debate between the proponents of tender panels and those of sole placing agency was strongly worded, it pales in comparison to the arguments between banks over whether the euronote – and a little later the Euro-commercial paper

Table 12
Britoil plc: Tender panel results

Date of issue	Total requested $m	Total bid $m	Amount over-subscribed $m	% over-subscribed	Maturity period	Lowest margin	Highest margin	Average
28.11.84	25.0	218	193	772%	181 days	−0.0075%	−0.0075%	−0.0075%
14.12.84	25.0	95	70	280%	90 days	+0.0250%	+0.0350%	+0.0290%
14.02.85	25.0	137	112	448%	181 days	−0.0250%	−0.0250%	−0.0250%
02.04.85	25.0	160	135	540%	91 days	−0.0550%	−0.0550%	−0.0550%
28.05.85	25.0	130	105	420%	92 days	−0.0650%	−0.0650%	−0.0650%
02.07.85	25.0	155	130	520%	92 days	−0.0650%	−0.0700%	−0.0672%
15.07.85	25.0	175	150	600%	92 days	−0.0830%	−0.0830%	−0.0830%
14.08.85	25.0	185	160	640%	92 days	−0.0626%	−0.0700%	−0.0677%
28.08.85	25.0	195	170	680%	93 days	−0.0400%	−0.0500%	−0.0480%
02.10.85	15.0	75	60	400%	30 days	−0.0400%	−0.0500%	−0.0433%
02.10.85	10.0	65	55	550%	61 days	−0.0400%	−0.0500%	−0.0450%
15.10.85	25.0	175	150	600%	92 days	−0.0350%	−0.0550%	−0.0424%
01.11.85	15.0	140	125	833%	31 days	−0.0400%	−0.0500%	−0.0467%
14.11.85	25.0	140	115	460%	32 days	−0.0400%	−0.0500%	−0.0460%
29.11.85	25.0	75	50	200%	45 days	−0.0390%	−0.0500%	−0.0400%
02.12.85	25.0	118	93	372%	63 days	−0.0350%	−0.0400%	−0.0390%
16.12.85	25.0	124	99	396%	60 days	−0.0310%	−0.0400%	−0.0346%
13.01.86	25.0	140	115	460%	29 days	−0.0400%	−0.0500%	−0.0430%
03.02.86	25.0	120	95	380%	28 days	−0.0458%	−0.0500%	−0.0481%
11.02.86	25.0	105	80	320%	28 days	−0.0468%	−0.0500%	−0.0488%
14.02.86	25.0	145	120	480%	28 days	−0.0500%	−0.0500%	−0.0500%
03.03.86	25.0	122	97	388%	31 days	−0.0465%	−0.0500%	−0.0481%
11.03.86	25.0	125	100	400%	30 days	−0.0463%	−0.0500%	−0.0486%
14.03.86	25.0	148	123	492%	31 days	−0.0500%	−0.0500%	−0.0500%
03.04.86	25.0	140	115	460%	29 days	−0.0500%	−0.0500%	−0.0540%
10.04.86	25.0	170	145	580%	29 days	−0.0610%	−0.0610%	−0.0610%
14.04.86	25.0	115	90	360%	30 days	−0.0500%	−0.0602%	−0.0540%
25.04.86	25.0	130	105	420%	91 days	−0.0400%	−0.0503%	−0.0459%
02.05.86	25.0	135	110	440%	31 days	−0.0500%	−0.0510%	−0.0503%
09.05.86	25.0	125	100	400%	31 days	−0.0472%	−0.0503%	−0.0495%
14.05.86	25.0	113	88	352%	30 days	−0.0422%	−0.0485%	−0.0454%
02.06.86	25.0	120	95	380%	30 days	−0.0412%	−0.0500%	−0.0473%
09.06.86	25.0	105	80	320%	30 days	−0.0420%	−0.0520%	−0.0481%
13.06.86	25.0	130	105	420%	31 days	−0.0400%	−0.0550%	−0.0474%
	815.0	4,550	3,725	4,580				

Accepted margin on LIBID

Table 13

THE KINGDOM OF SWEDEN TENDER PANEL RESULTS (US$ MILLIONS)

Amount Requested	Amount Taken	Period	Best Bid	Last Accepted	Weighted Average	Total Bids Received
DLR 200	DLR 200	29.11.84 TO 28.02.85	(0.3500)	(0.1356)	(0.1483)	DLR 1,823
DLR 300	DLR 300	17.12.84 TO 18.03.85	(0.1700)	(0.0900)	(0.1131)	DLR 1,599
DLR 200	DLR 200	04.02.85 TO 07.05.85	(0.0800)	(0.0626)	(0.0745)	DLR 1,105
DLR 200	DLR 200	11.02.85 TO 13.05.85	(0.0800)	(0.0307)	(0.0533)	DLR 953
DLR 200	DLR 200	28.02.85 TO 31.05.85	(0.0800)	(0.0209)	(0.0482)	DLR 740
DLR 200	DLR 200	07.03.85 TO 09.09.85	(0.0500)	(0.0000)	(0.0105)	DLR 516
DLR 300	DLR 300	18.03.85 TO 18.04.85	(0.0710)	(0.0410)	(0.0566)	DLR 902.5
DLR 200	DLR 200	18.04.85 TO 18.07.85	(0.0700)	(0.0109)	(0.0332)	DLR 629
DLR 300	DLR 300	13.05.85 TO 13.08.85	(0.0800)	(0.0200)	(0.0367)	DLR 820
DLR 200	DLR 200	31.05.85 TO 28.06.85	(0.0100)	(0.0400)	(0.0606)	DLR 995
DLR 200	DLR 200	29.06.85 TO 31.12.85	(0.0508)	(0.0300)	(0.0421)	DLR 859
DLR 100	DLR 100	18.07.85 TO 18.10.85	(0.0700)	(0.0509)	(0.0628)	DLR 711
DLR 100	DLR 100	18.07.85 TO 21.01.86	(0.0609)	(0.0400)	(0.0488)	DLR 547
DLR 100	DLR 100	13.08.85 TO 13.11.85	(0.0890)	(0.0591)	(0.0655)	DLR 961
DLR 200	DLR 200	09.09.85 TO 09.12.85	(0.0802)	(0.0550)	(0.0658)	DLR 636
DLR 200	DLR 200	08.10.85 TO 08.01.86	(0.0890)	(0.0571)	(0.06087)	DLR 855
DLR 200	DLR 200	18.10.85 TO 18.11.85	(0.0895)	(0.0572)	(0.0748)	DLR 825
DLR 200	DLR 200	18.11.85 TO 18.02.86	(0.0801)	(0.0550)	(0.0647)	DLR 930
DLR 200	DLR 200	09.12.85 TO 09.03.86	(0.0800)	(0.0619)	(0.0459)	DLR 385
DLR 200	DLR 200	08.01.86 TO 08.04.86	(0.0605)	(0.0500)	(0.0554)	DLR 765
DLR 100	DLR 100	21.01.86 TO 31.04.86	(0.0701)	(0.0701)	(0.0701)	DLR 660
DLR 200	DLR 200	28.01.86 TO 28.02.86	(0.1000)	(0.0550)	(0.0643)	DLR 830
DLR 200	DLR 200	18.02.86 TO 18.03.86	(0.0810)	(0.0560)	(0.0631)	DLR 905
DLR 200	DLR 200	28.02.86 TO 28.05.86	(0.0885)	(0.0510)	(0.0623)	DLR 676
DLR 200	DLR 200	10.03.86 TO 10.09.86	(0.0790)	(0.0600)	(0.0500)	DLR 340
DLR 200	DLR 200	18.03.86 TO 18.06.86	(0.0790)	(0.0510)	(0.0587)	DLR 685
DLR 100	DLR 100	08.04.86 TO 08.07.85	(0.0850)	(0.0551)	(0.0682)	DLR 660
DLR 100	DLR 100	21.04.86 TO 21.07.86	(0.0910)	(0.0650)	(0.0724)	DLR 443
DLR 100	DLR 100	06.05.86 TO 06.08.86	(0.0830)	(0.0710)	(0.0750)	DLR 635
DLR 100	DLR 100	28.05.86 TO 28.08.86	(0.0910)	(0.0790)	(0.0864)	DLR 558
DLR 100	DLR 100	18.06.86 TO 18.09.86	(0.0910)	(0.0900)	(0.0953)	DLR 612
DLR 100	DLR 100	08.07.86 TO 08.10.86	(0.124)	(0.114)	(0.118)	DLR 700
DLR 100	DLR 100	21.07.86 TO 21.10.86	(0.132)	(0.120)	(0.125)	DLR 845

All bids expressed as a margin below LIBID

market was a trading or a placement market. Let us analyse what we mean by these terms.

Placement is quite straightforward. A working definition might be the sale of primary euronotes to investors whose expected behaviour is to hold them until maturity. It implies that euronotes are issued at a yield reasonable enough to allow the investor to obtain a fair return whilst at the same time allowing the selling bank a reasonable sales commission. Trading does not imply a primary market, rather a secondary market. Most issuers were persuaded that euronote issuance facilities would offer not only a consistently low cost but the opportunity to have their paper placed with new investors thereby widening their sources of finance. A number of banks took a strict view of these objectives and sought to develop a non-bank investor base upon which they could call when an issue of euronotes was announced. Such banks would consult with those investors, make a bid on the tender panel and, if successful, then seek to place that paper immediately with those investors. This depended on a lot of 'ifs': would an investor originally agree to buy paper at an agreed margin over/under LIBOR? Would the bid be successful? Would the investor still be willing to buy at the same yield if the bid was successful? After a number of unsuccessful bids would the bank lose credibility in its investors' eyes? Here, once again, are the problems inherent in the tender panel structure. The unreliability of the process as to firm supply of paper meant that the development of an investor base was difficult. It can be argued that the tender panel made placement very difficult to achieve and forced banks into trading.

Trading, therefore can be seen to be the buying and selling of euronotes between professional institutions without specifically targeting sales at end investors willing to hold the paper until maturity. This is very much akin to the practice of the CD market and a number of banks actually handled their euronote sales through their CD traders. Trading does not seek as a first priority to achieve the objective of diversifying the issuer's sources of finance. Buyers tend to be other professional banks who will also seek to on-sell the paper when they see a profit opportunity. Trading banks were willing to make and wanted to receive a bid-offer quotation in all major euronote issues. Placement banks would never offer paper to trading banks.

All money market instruments benefit from an actively-traded secondary market in order to provide liquidity for all participants, investors and banks alike. Criticism in 1984 and 1985 was levelled at banks actively trading euronotes that this did nothing to achieve firm placement and led to inconsistent yield levels. In short, it was felt that a secondary market pointed to the absence of a primary market. Let us consider an example of this:

Example 7

Bank A obtained in a tender panel $5 million of 90-day euronotes at LIBID less 0.06% p a. At the rate-fixing LIBID was set at 6.50% p a, thus Bank A owns the paper at 6.44% p a. The euronotes run from 3 June to 1 September.

Using the discount note calculation in Chapter 1, Bank A paid to the issuer on 3 June:

$$\frac{5,000,000}{1 + \left(\dfrac{6.44 \times 90}{36000}\right)}$$

$$= \$4,920,775.51$$

This amount represents an asset on Bank A's books and requires to be funded. As Bank A expects to sell the euronotes quite quickly it simply funds in the overnight market where borrowing rates are 6.50% p a.

Bank A therefore borrows \$4,920,775.51 at 6.50% p a for 1 day (3 June until 4 June), incurring a borrowing cost of \$888.47. This represents a negative 'carry' on its holding of euronotes because the accruing income on that holding is:

$$\frac{\$4,920,775.51 \times 6.44}{36000}$$

$$= \$880.27$$

The differential is not just \$8.20 per day (\$888.47–\$880.27) because if interest rates stay constant it will rise when Bank A comes to renew its borrowing. The frequency of that renewal is critical since, for example, if Bank A funded the holding with overnight borrowings for a prolonged period, the compound interest effect would become very expensive. It is not within the scope of this book to analyse in depth how money market instruments are traded and funded but it is enough to say that how long to fund and at what point to buy and sell are among the most important and complex decisions a money market dealer has to make. Funding is a risk business and any value in the euronote holding can be lost by incorrect funding decisions.

To take our illustrative example one step further, Bank A for value on 4 June wishes to sell the euronotes and repay its overnight borrowing. Because interest rates fall on that day and LIBID now stands at 6.375% p a, Bank A is now able to sell its holding at, say, 6.41% p a, i e at LIBID plus 0.035% p a.

It receives therefore for that sale:

$$\frac{5,000,000}{1 + \left(\dfrac{6.41 \times 89}{36000}\right)}$$

$$= \$4,922,001.32$$

Its total profit from the buying and selling operation is:

$$\$4,922,001.32 - (\$4,920,775.51 + 888.47)$$

$$= \$337.34$$

The important factor which allowed Bank A to make a profit on the above transaction was its ability to place the paper at 6.41% p a, three basis points below the level it had bought the paper the previous day. This may have been due to one or both of the following reasons:

(i) because it had been awarded paper in the tender panel at an unaggressive yield for the quality of that issuer; or

(ii) because interest rates fell between purchase and sale rendering the euronote holding more valuable relative to other instruments in the market.

If LIBID had not fallen from 6.50% p a to 6.375% p a in the above example but had stayed at the same level and, furthermore, if Bank A had cut out its euronote position at the same margin (0.035% p a) above LIBID, it would have actually made a loss on the transaction:

$$\text{Sale of euronotes} = \frac{5,000,000}{1 + \left(\dfrac{6.535 \times 89}{36000}\right)}$$

$$= \$4,920,504.47$$

less purchase of notes = $4,920,775.51
less funding cost = $888.47
total loss = ($1,159.51)

It is therefore apparent that if banks bid very aggressively in tender panels, right at the limit of market value for an issuer's name, profit can only come from changes in interest rates or from the yield curve remaining positive.

Banks are bidding out any intrinsic value in the paper and have to rely on factors beyond their control (i e interest rates) to add value. Indeed, position-taking in euronotes in expectation of a fall in interest rates became a widespread practice in the euronote market from 1984 onwards. It was often forced on banks irrespective of their tendency towards placement or trading because the tender panel distribution method provoked such aggressive bidding that euronotes were simply too expensive for investors to buy.

The interest rate environment from 1984 onwards helped the practice of positioning euronotes to flourish. From the third quarter of 1984 to the present day, Eurodollar interest rates have, with brief interludes of small rises, fallen dramatically.

Table 14

Average Eurodollar interbank offered rates

	1984	*1985*	*1986**
1-month LIBOR	10.56	8.24	7.50
3-month LIBOR	10.85	8.40	7.46

Source: SBCI   *until June

Table 14 shows that the fall during this period has been over 300 basis points for both one-month maturities and for three-month maturities. Moreover, the yield curve has almost always been positive (except for recent months) which has meant that banks have normally been able to fund purchases of longer-maturity paper profitably with shorter-maturity borrowings.

Whilst a falling interest rate environment helped both placement banks and trading banks, it helped the latter most. The perceived risk of bidding aggressively for euronotes and holding them against a fall in interest rates was low enough to encourage active position-taking. The placement bank might tend to take short-term inventory positions until an investor could be found for the paper but generally it did not seek an external market event to restore value to the paper being held. Trading banks, however, were very often responsible for aggressive, better-than-market bids and they required a shift in interest rates to create value in the paper. Positions were then traded actively amongst a group of market professionals.

Trading therefore did little to achieve the objective of developing an investor base for an issuer's euronotes. Somewhat perversely some banks were claiming successful tender panel allotments as proof of placement power when inter-professional trading was their real market for the paper. This claim might of course impress present and future issuers to assist in obtaining profitable mandates. It also created in issuers' minds confusion about who was doing what in the market. As long as their tender panel bids were aggressive and hence their cost of borrowing low, issuers did not seem to mind what went on behind the scenes.

One criticism of position-taking was that it led to inconsistent and ultimately higher yield levels for issuers. In Example 7 above Bank A buys paper at LIBID and sells it at LIBID plus 0.035% p a and makes a profit because LIBID changes as interest rates fall. It is argued that if this consistently occurs, then investors will come to set the expected return on this issuer's paper at LIBID plus 0.035% p a. If interest rates were expected to remain flat or even rise, Bank A will not bid at below LIBID to obtain paper in the tender panel but, in order to make a turn, might bid at LIBID plus 0.05% p a. This is a logical criticism though it must be said that major borrowers, despite warnings that their issuing yield might suffer, did not really see a deterioration in cost. Some borrowers, however, did but not to the extent that position-taking could be accused of having a marked effect on market yields. Care must be taken when referring to LIBID since in absolute rate terms it may not be the same for every party involved in a particular transaction. Euronote dealers buy and sell euronotes in the market on an absolute interest rate basis paying little attention to LIBID/LIBOR once the rate fixing is accomplished. The focus on LIBID/LIBOR comes from tender panels where all bidding is tied to these benchmarks. There is little evidence that investors actively compare absolute euronote yields offered to them with LIBID rather than with the absolute yields on other alternative investment instruments. The LIBID benchmark can at times be a confusing and irrelevant factor in the Euro-commercial paper market.

The placement versus trading debate was not really solved in the sense that a specific category of bank clearly won the argument. To be fair, the argument at times became confused as the terms 'placing' and 'trading' were often misconstrued by different banks. The euronote market – and later the Euro-commercial paper market – recognised that whilst placement is of principal importance some kind of trading was required in order to provide liquidity. Whilst some banks claim that inter-professional trading creates that important element of liquidity which underpins the market for the investor, others feel that it is merely an absence of a placement capability with end-investors. Placement banks recognise the need for liquidity but apply it properly to their investors. The term 'liquidity support' is increasingly used and means that a bank which has sold a euronote to an investor will always be prepared to repurchase it at a fair market price. This assures the investor that it can always obtain its principal before maturity. Liquidity support as opposed to a fully-traded secondary market has now become a feature of the euronote and Euro-commercial paper market.

CHAPTER 5

The advent of Euro-commercial paper programmes

By early 1985 the debate in the market shifted away from the relative merits of particular distribution methods to individual banks' performance at placing euronotes. The implicit recognition was that at last a market of significant size and liquidity had established itself. The role of banks as placers of euronotes came under scrutiny not only by issuers but by their own competitors. With the emphasis now firmly on the placement of euronotes the rigidities and inflexibilities of existing distribution methods became all too apparent. These methods, since they formed part of a committed, syndicated facility, involved several banks and required the lengthy administrative procedures and constraints as to amount and frequency of offering described earlier in chapter 4. Moreover, these methods dictated that offerings of euronotes were 'issuer-led' rather than 'investor-led'. Given that a minimum of four or five days was required to issue euronotes and that the entire tender panel process had to be activated, no bank could realistically reflect an investor's preferences to an issuer and expect them to be accommodated quickly and simply. Issuers selected by and large the amounts and maturities which suited them. Indeed, as suggested previously, this fact led to banks having to take positions in euronotes and to seek to place with investors afterwards or to trade with other banks.

Existing distribution methods made it almost impossible to develop a stable, satisfied investor base. Supply of paper was just too unreliable. Banks, innovative as ever, began very quickly to propose solutions to this problem. Not unnaturally, the nature of the product led them to look westward to the domestic commercial paper market, as had been the case in the early 1970s and in 1980 with the Associates programme. The size of the domestic commercial paper market had grown in 1985 to over $250 billion in outstandings. Foreign issuers (of which a number had arranged euronote issuance facilities) had over $35 billion outstanding in the first half of 1985, almost 15% of the market. Commercial paper issuance methodology was familiar to bank and borrower alike (indeed many foreign banks already issued domestic commercial paper) and it was logical that the euronote market should take up that model and call it the Euro-commercial paper programme.

The model is simple and is virtually identical to the Euro-commercial paper programmes of earlier years. The borrower appoints a dealer (or dealers) to a programme which is uncommitted, ie it is not coupled with a commercial bank underwriting commitment. The borrower will as a matter of prudence have back-up lines of credit but they will be a separate arrangement from the programme. Under the programme the dealer's responsibility is to place the issuer's notes[1] with end investors and to develop an investor base which will form a consistent and competitive source of funds.

The earliest programmes to be set up at this time comprised mainly corporate borrowers. Norsk Hydro signed its two-dealer $200 million programme in March 1985. ITT Financial Corporation was the first US issuer to establish a programme (21 June) and BOC Group plc, the first UK issuer (31 July). By the middle of that summer some 20 programmes had been established. Normally a programme was accompanied by an information memorandum (or an investor memorandum) which assisted the investor in its credit decision. An example is shown below.

Somewhat perversely, the Euro-commercial paper programme is a throwback to the objectives and practice of the sole placing agency distribution method. It puts the onus on one bank (or a very small group of banks) to develop an investor base for the issuer's notes. This bank (ie the dealer) is responsible for maintaining a consistent yield and an orderly market in the notes, just like the sole placing agent. It is expected to demonstrate good performance in good and bad markets alike. The Euro-commercial paper programme avoids the rigidities of the euronote issuance facility to which sole placing agency was tied. With the exigencies of syndicating a committed facility no longer applicable, the Euro-commercial paper programme really became the most flexible note distribution method in the market. In practice, initially, issuers could use three basic techniques for issuing paper under such programmes:

COMPETITIVE BIDDING

Dealers are asked to bid for a tranche of notes which the issuer plans to issue that day. The dealer(s) bidding the lowest yield obtains the notes and proceeds to place them with investors.

This, of course, is similar to a miniature tender panel and has all the drawbacks and disadvantages of that method which have been reviewed at length in earlier chapters. Although, typically, the issuer would ask for bids at, say, 10.30 am two days before issue date and award them by 10.45 am the same morning, dealers are still uncertain as to their supply of paper and therefore still cannot make firm offers to their investors prior to the bidding process, (it should be noted that the market still works on a two-day forward settlement basis). Moreover, although the issuer can and will consult with its dealers on the optimum amount and maturity for prevailing market conditions, this practice is still largely an issuer-led approach imposing the issuer's own amount and maturity requirements rather than the investor's. It risks therefore not satisfying proper investor demand and the dealers' desire to service their investors.

1 We will use the term 'note' to designate the instrument issued under an uncommitted programme as opposed to 'euronote' which is the instrument issued pursuant to a committed euronote issuance facility. The actual instruments are legally identical and look the same but each is issued under different distribution methods.

THE BOC GROUP

///////////////////////////////

US$ 200 000 000
EURO COMMERCIAL PAPER PROGRAMME

1 SUMMARY OF THE TERMS OF THE PROGRAMME

The BOC Group, Inc. (the "Issuer") incorporated in the State of Nevada, USA has appointed Credit Suisse First Boston Limited, Salomon Brothers International Limited and Swiss Bank Corporation International Limited, as dealers (the "Dealers") in connection with a programme for the issue of its short-term promissory notes (the "Notes") which will be unconditionally and irrevocably guaranteed by The BOC Group plc (the "Guarantor"). The Notes will have the following terms:

- Form — Bearer Promissory Notes.

- Denomination — US $500 000.

- Interest — The Notes will not bear interest but will be sold at a discount.

- Maturity — Any period to a maximum of 6 months (183 days).

- Restrictions on sale — The Notes will not be registered under the Securities Act of 1933 of the United States of America. The Notes may not be offered or sold in the United States or to nationals or residents thereof other than to foreign branches of US banks (as stated in the Notes).

- Withholding Taxes — Payments on the Notes to holders who are not US persons (as defined in the Notes) will, subject to the exceptions and limitations set forth on the reverse of the Notes, be made free and clear of United States withholding tax.

Swiss Bank Corporation will act as Issuing Agent and Principal Paying Agent for the Notes through its offices at Aeschenvorstadt 1, 4002 Basle, Switzerland and 99 Gresham Street, London. Banque Internationale à Luxembourg S.A. will act as Sub-paying Agent through its office at 2 Boulevard Royal, 2935 Luxembourg.

This Information Memorandum contains summary information concerning the Notes, the Issuer, and the Guarantor. It does not constitute an offer or invitation to subscribe for or purchase any Notes. Further information is available from:

Credit Suisse First Boston Limited
Agency Department, 22 Bishopsgate, London EC2N 4BW: (01) 634 3000

Salomon Brothers International Limited
Money Markets Group, 1 Angel Court, London EC2R 7HS: (01) 600 9171

Swiss Bank Corporation International Limited
Euronotes Desk, Three Keys House, 130 Wood Street, London EC2V 6AQ: (01) 606 0902

1

As at the date hereof The BOC Group plc confirms that the summary information in this Information Memorandum when construed in conjunction with the 1985 Report and Accounts concerning it and its subsidiaries is accurate in all material respects and warrants that since the publication of those Accounts there has been no such change in the financial condition or operations of The BOC Group plc and its subsidiaries taken as a whole as might reasonably be expected materially and adversely to affect the decision of a person considering whether to purchase Notes.

Potential purchasers should determine for themselves the relevance of the information contained in this Information Memorandum as supplemented from time to time and their interest in the purchase of the Notes should be based upon such investigation as they deem necessary.

The Dealers do not make any representation, express or implied, as to the accuracy or completeness of any of the information in this Information Memorandum.

2 THE BOC GROUP

The BOC Group plc, the Guarantor of the Notes, was incorporated in England in 1886. The BOC Group, Inc., the Issuer of the Notes, is one of The BOC Group plc's principal wholly-owned subsidiaries.

The BOC Group operates in some 50 countries throughout the world. In each of these countries it manufactures and markets one or more of its major product lines: industrial gases and related products, health care products and services, and carbon-based products. In all these fields the Group is either a world leader or among the world's major producers.

The gases businesses principally produce and distribute oxygen, nitrogen, argon, rare atmospheric gases, fuel gases, carbon dioxide, special gases and gas mixtures. These products are essential to a great many industrial processes and are sold to a wide range of customers in the chemical, oil, food, electronics, metal fabrication, steel and other industries. Over the years the Group has been very successful in finding and developing new applications for its industrial gases.

The Group has a number of substantial health care businesses. Anaquest, in the US, manufactures and sells anaesthetic pharmaceuticals. Ohmeda is a world leader in supplying integrated anaesthesia systems and equipment for use in operating theatres. Glasrock Home Health Care is one of the largest home oxygen therapy businesses in the US providing a range of health care products to patients in their own homes through a network of over 250 branches. Viggo, based in Europe, manufactures a wide range of intravenous products.

The carbon businesses manufacture graphite electrodes for use in electric arc steel furnaces, and a wide range of graphite speciality products for such uses as carbon battery electrodes, motor and generator brushes, crucibles, moulds and rocket nozzles.

The Group also has significant interests in the manufacture of carbide; vacuum pumps and equipment for the semiconductor and other industries; architectural and environmental glass coating; food distribution; and educational services.

A summary of the recent financial history of The BOC Group plc and its subsidiaries is shown in the facing table. The annual financial data has been abridged from the full group accounts. The accounts for 1980 to 1985 each received an unqualified auditors' report and have been delivered to the Registrar of Companies.

3   FINANCIAL RESULTS OF THE BOC GROUP plc

The Group's accounting policies are based on the Modified Historical Cost Convention which permits the revaluation of fixed assets.

(£ million)

Group Results	1980	1981	1982	1983	1984	1985
			Year to 30 September			
Turnover	1194.5	1521.7	1534.2	1701.6	2103.0	1900.9
Trading profit*	119.5	159.3	163.2	155.7	221.9	243.2
Interest (net)	(55.1)	(64.2)	(60.6)	(59.9)	(84.1)	(71.9)
Profit before tax	64.4	95.1	102.6	95.8	137.8	171.3
Tax	(17.3)	(37.6)	(27.6)	(23.8)	(44.1)	(49.9)
Attributable to minorities	(7.3)	(11.2)	(10.5)	(17.2)	(14.4)	(11.8)
Earnings	39.8	46.3	64.5	54.8	79.3	109.6
Extraordinary items	(10.6)	0.6	6.1	(12.8)	12.5	(7.1)

Trading profit is after charging depreciation on a current cost basis.

Condensed Balance Sheets	1980	1981	1982	1983	1984	1985
			At 30 September			
Employment of Capital						
Tangible fixed assets†	899.7	1152.6	1277.6	1568.7	1762.0	1532.7
Related coys./other investments	29.5	43.9	71.4	126.3	130.9	142.9
Working capital (excluding cash, deposits and short term borrowings)	244.0	278.4	300.3	259.0	358.7	333.0
	1173.2	1474.9	1649.3	1954.0	2251.6	2008.6
Capital employed						
Shareholders' capital & reserves	585.9	787.0	883.0	1037.4	1199.8	1124.8
Minority shareholders' interests	79.4	101.0	103.0	127.5	142.6	108.7
	665.3	888.0	986.0	1164.9	1342.4	1233.5
Non current liabilities and provisions	34.5	70.7	74.0	81.4	110.6	113.8
Net borrowings & finance leases	473.4	516.2	589.3	707.7	798.6	661.3
	1173.2	1474.9	1649.3	1954.0	2251.6	2008.6

†At replacement cost or economic value if lower.*

4   DISTRIBUTION OF THE INFORMATION MEMORANDUM

The Notes may not be offered or sold in Great Britain by means of this Information Memorandum or any other document other than to persons whose ordinary business it is to buy or sell shares or debentures, whether as principal or agent, otherwise than in circumstances which do not constitute an offer to the public within the meaning of the Companies Act 1985, and neither this Information Memorandum nor any other document relating to the Notes may be distributed in or from Great Britain (except by persons permitted to do so under the securities laws of Great Britain) otherwise than to persons whose business involves the acquisition and disposal, or the holding, of securities (whether as principal or as agent).

The distribution of this Information Memorandum and the offering of the Notes in certain jurisdictions may be restricted by law and persons into whose possession this Information Memorandum comes are required by the Issuer and the Dealers to inform themselves about and to observe any such restrictions. No application will be made at any time to list the Notes on any stock exchange.

5 SPECIMEN FORM OF NOTE (FRONT)

THE BOC GROUP, INC.

(Incorporated with limited liability in the State of Nevada in the United States of America)

Serial No: Issue Date:

Amount: **U.S.$500,000**   Maturity Date:

For value received, **The BOC Group, Inc.** (the "Issuer") hereby unconditionally promises to pay to the bearer the principal amount of:

U.S.$500,000 (five hundred thousand United States Dollars)

on the Maturity Date shown above, in accordance with the terms and conditions hereof. Payment will be made only against surrender of this Note at the offices of Swiss Bank Corporation at Aeschenvorstadt 1, 4002 Basle, Switzerland or 99 Gresham Street, London EC2P 2BR, England or at the office of Banque Internationale à Luxembourg S.A., 2 Boulevard Royal, 2953 Luxembourg, the Paying Agents of the Issuer. Payment will be made by cheque or draft drawn on a bank in New York City mailed to an address outside the United States, or by wire transfer to a U.S. Dollar account outside the United States.

Reference is hereby made to the further provisions on the reverse hereof, which form part of this Note.

This Note and the Guarantee referred to below are governed by and shall be construed in accordance with the law of England.

This Note shall not be valid for any purpose until the Certificate of Authentication enfaced hereon shall have been duly signed on behalf of Swiss Bank Corporation, Basle, as Issuing Agent.

IN WITNESS WHEREOF the Issuer has caused this Note to be duly executed in facsimile on its behalf.

THE BOC GROUP, INC.

By

(Authorised Signatory)

GUARANTEE BY THE BOC GROUP plc

The obligations of the Issuer in respect of this Note are unconditionally and irrevocably guaranteed by **The BOC Group plc** (a company incorporated in England with limited liability) under a Guarantee dated 31 July 1985 (the "Guarantee"). Copies of the Guarantee are available for inspection at the offices of the Paying Agents.

Certificate of Authentication
SWISS BANK CORPORATION

By

(Authorised Signatory)
Without recourse, warranty or liability

THIS NOTE HAS NOT BEEN AND WILL NOT BE REGISTERED UNDER THE SECURITIES ACT OF 1933 OF THE UNITED STATES OF AMERICA AND IS NOT BEING, AND MAY NOT BE, OFFERED, SOLD, RESOLD OR DELIVERED, EXCEPT IN ACCORDANCE WITH CERTAIN RESTRICTIONS AS SET FORTH BELOW, IN THE UNITED STATES (WHICH TERM MEANS THE UNITED STATES OF AMERICA, THE COMMONWEALTH OF PUERTO RICO AND EACH TERRITORY AND POSSESSION OF THE UNITED STATES OF AMERICA AND ALL AREAS SUBJECT TO ITS JURISDICTION) OR TO NATIONALS OR RESIDENTS THEREOF, INCLUDING THE ESTATE OF ANY SUCH PERSON, AND ANY CORPORATION, PARTNERSHIP OR OTHER ENTITY CREATED OR ORGANIZED IN OR UNDER THE LAWS OF THE UNITED STATES OR ANY POLITICAL SUBDIVISION THEREOF (ALL OF THE FOREGOING BEING "U.S. PERSONS"), AND ANY OFFER, SALE, RESALE OR DELIVERY OF THIS NOTE IN THE UNITED STATES OR TO U.S. PERSONS (OTHER THAN IN ACCORDANCE WITH SUCH RESTRICTIONS) MAY CONSTITUTE A VIOLATION OF UNITED STATES LAW UNLESS SUCH OFFER, SALE, RESALE OR DELIVERY IS MADE IN COMPLIANCE WITH THE REGISTRATION REQUIREMENTS OF THE SECURITIES ACT OF 1933 OF THE UNITED STATES OF AMERICA OR PURSUANT TO AN EXEMPTION THEREFROM. BY ITS ACCEPTANCE OF THIS NOTE AND BY PRESENTING IT FOR PAYMENT, THE HOLDER HEREOF REPRESENTS AND WARRANTS THAT (I) IT IS NOT A U.S. PERSON OTHER THAN A BRANCH LOCATED OUTSIDE THE UNITED STATES OF A NATIONAL BANKING ASSOCIATION ORGANIZED UNDER THE LAWS OF THE UNITED STATES, OR A BRANCH LOCATED OUTSIDE THE UNITED STATES OF A BANKING INSTITUTION ORGANIZED UNDER THE LAWS OF ANY STATE OR TERRITORY OF THE UNITED STATES OR THE DISTRICT OF COLUMBIA, THE BUSINESS OF WHICH IS SUBSTANTIALLY CONFINED TO BANKING AND IS SUPERVISED BY THE STATE OR TERRITORIAL BANKING COMMISSION OR SIMILAR OFFICIAL (EACH OF THE FOREGOING BEING A "FOREIGN BRANCH"), AND (II) IT IS NOT ACTING FOR OR ON BEHALF OF A U.S. PERSON OTHER THAN A FOREIGN BRANCH.

6   SPECIMEN FORM OF NOTE (BACK)

1. The Issuer will, subject to the exceptions and limitations set forth below, pay as additional interest on this Note such additional amounts as are necessary in order that the net payment by the Issuer or a Paying Agent of the principal of, including original issue discount, if any, and deemed interest, if any, on, this Note to a holder who is not a United States person (as defined below), after deduction for any present or future tax, assessment or governmental charge of the United States (as defined below), or a political subdivision or taxing authority thereof or therein, required to be withheld or deducted by the Issuer or a Paying Agent from the payment, will not be less than the amount provided in this Note to be then due and payable; *provided, however,* that the foregoing obligation to pay additional amounts shall not apply:—

   (a) to a tax, assessment or governmental charge that is imposed or deducted solely by reason of a connection of the holder with the United States other than the mere holding of this Note or the mere receipt of the payment;

   (b) to a tax, assessment or governmental charge that is imposed or deducted solely by reason of the holder, if required, failing to establish that the holder is not a United States person or is not subject to United States backup withholding tax with respect to the payment;

   (c) to a tax, assessment or governmental charge that is imposed or deducted solely by reason of a change in law that becomes effective more than 15 days after the payment becomes due or is duly provided for, whichever occurs later;

   (d) to a tax, assessment or governmental charge that is payable otherwise than by withholding or deduction by the Issuer or a Paying Agent from the payment;

   (e) to a tax, assessment or governmental charge that is imposed solely by reason of a holder being a "10-percent shareholder" of the Issuer as defined in section 871(h)(3) of the United States Internal Revenue Code;

   (f) to an estate, inheritance, gift, sales, transfer, wealth or personal property tax or a similar tax, assessment or governmental charge;

   (g) to a holder that is not the beneficial owner of the Note, or a portion thereof, or that is a foreign partnership, but only to the extent that a beneficial owner or member of the partnership would not have been entitled to the payment of an additional amount had the beneficial owner or member received directly its beneficial or distributive share of the payment; or

   (h) to a tax, assessment or governmental charge that is imposed by reason of a combination of the foregoing.

   Payments on this Note are subject in all cases to any tax, fiscal or other law applicable thereto. Except as provided in the preceding paragraph, the Issuer is not required to make any payment with respect to any tax, assessment or governmental charge imposed by any government or a political subdivision or taxing authority thereof or therein.

   For the purposes of the foregoing, (i) "United States person" means an individual who, as to the United States, is a citizen or resident of the United States, an estate or trust that is subject to United States Federal income taxation without regard to the source of its income, or a corporation, partnership or other entity created or organized in or under the laws of the United States or any political subdivision thereof; and (ii) "United States" means the United States of America, the Commonwealth of Puerto Rico and each territory and possession of the United States of America and all areas subject to its jurisdiction.

2. If the date specified as the Maturity Date is not a day on which commercial banks and foreign exchange markets are open for business in London and New York City (a "Business Day"), the Maturity Date shall be the next succeeding day which is a Business Day (unless such next succeeding Business Day is in the next calendar month or would thereby cause the Maturity Date to be more than 183 days after the Issue Date, in either of which events the Maturity Date shall be the immediately preceding day that is a Business Day).

PROTECTED AMOUNTS

Some issuers divide a tranch of notes to be offered equally between the dealers at the same yield. This is effected in the spirit of wide and fair distribution but requires that the yield be agreed between the dealers, (somewhat akin to the issuer-set margin approach discussed earlier). Whilst in principle it seems an equitable approach, it has potential drawbacks. The consultation process to determine the agreed yield can take too long. In an environment of continuing fierce competition a dealer may endeavour to impress the borrower by quoting highly aggressive, potentially unsustainable yields or complaining that its allocation or protected amount is too small and thus damaging its attempts to develop fully the issuer's name with investors. With careful selection of dealers with commensurate placement capabilities and a willingness to work together, a sensible, co-ordinated dealership arrangement can be constructed.

This method is honourable in its intentions and in the early months of a programme it can assure dealers of their all-important supply of paper. Issuers argue that it allows dealers to establish their placement channels, market the issuer's name effectively and goes some way to assuring wide distribution.

UNSOLICITED BIDS OR DIRECT BIDDING

This quite simply describes the process whereby a dealer will call the issuer and bid directly for a certain amount of notes for a certain maturity at a certain rate. The issuer may not in this case have signalled its intention to issue as it would with the first two techniques discussed, but may be persuaded to issue by the amount, maturity and rate contained in the dealer's unsolicited bid or bids.

Whereas the formalised nature of the previously discussed techniques tends to lead to even maturities (30, 60, 90 and 180 days) and are largely issuer-led, direct bidding is Euro-commercial paper in highly flexible, investor-led form. Dealers can often reflect to the issuer specific investor preferences as to maturity, especially 'broken period' maturities (eg 36 days or 99 days – not even months) and because of the particular importance these maturities might have for the investor the issuer can command a lower cost. Direct bidding requires issuers to adopt a more flexible approach to funding in order to derive the maximum cost benefit from a Euro-commercial paper programme. It may be more convenient for the issuer to issue $25 million all for 90 days but it may be cheaper if it agrees to meet an investor's specific preferences and issue say, $10 million for 85 days, $10 million for 93 days and $5 million for 99 days. Clearly there are times when the issuer has a very specific maturity date requirement and cannot show such flexibility but in general the more flexibility a programme can provide, the greater the potential for a lower cost.

COMMISSIONS

Some programmes include explicit commissions as remuneration for dealers whilst others work on a 'net-price' basis. The dealing commission is a feature of the domestic commercial paper market and has been adopted by a large minority of the Euro-commercial paper market. If, for example, the issuer posts a rate of 6.90% p a and the dealing commission is 0.075% p a, most often the applicable rate to the issuer would quite simply be 6.975% p a. In some cases, the commission is not calculated on each sale of notes but calculated on the average amount outstanding under the programme during, say, a three-month period and paid to the dealer quarterly in arrear.

It is argued that a commission paid at the time of sale is more easily 'manipulated' by the dealer. In the above example, the dealer could sell notes to an investor at 6.95% p a and merely take 0.025% p a commission; the issuer would not know. In cases where the commission is paid separately after a lapse of time it is more cumbersome and expensive for the dealer to use the commission to subsidise a sale of notes. It would effectively be giving the investor money now which would only be recouped in some months' time and during that period a loss may be shown on the dealer's books until receipt of the commission.

'Net price' quite simply means the quoting of a single yield to the issuer which would include a commission if the dealer so wishes. Thus, if an investor is willing to buy notes at 6.90% p a, the dealer has to weigh up what commission it should add in order to provide itself with satisfactory remuneration but at the same time ensure that the total yield is attractive enough for the issuer to issue notes. 6.975% p a might be considered by the dealer too expensive but 6.95% might represent an attractive level. A majority of issuers select the net price method on the simple psychological basis that in a competitive environment a dealer will tend to opt for a low implicit commission when bidding for notes.

LIQUIDITY SUPPORT AND ISSUANCE BEHAVIOUR

In the section entitled 'Trading versus placement' above the concept of liquidity support was analysed. The dealers under a Euro-commercial paper programme will commit to provide liquidity support in that they will always be prepared to make a bid-offer quote to the investor. The bid yield would be at a level so that the investor could come out of its investment at a fair current market level. This level might be the rate at which the issuer is prepared to issue paper on the day of repurchase. The convention of the Euro-commercial paper market is to quote a 0.05% p a spread, e g

			Bid	*Offer*
Kingdom of Sweden	$25m	8/9	6.85	6.80

The offer yield is that at which the dealer will *sell* notes *to* an investor, the bid yield is that it will *buy* notes *from* an investor. The '8/9' designation means that the $25 million tranche of notes matures on 8 September.

The Euro-commercial paper programmes first established in 1985 were designed really for intermittent, albeit fairly regular, use. Unlike their US counterparts, Euro-issuers did not use their programmes for constant, daily issuance. This was partly because the market would have found it difficult to handle the concentration of paper of one issuer that this approach might have produced. An average US issuer can easily have over $500 million of paper outstanding in the market at any one time and with an average maturity of less than 30 days the issuer could be repaying and reissuing $20–25 million per day. Another reason was that the typical note maturity of the Euro-commercial paper market was well in excess of that in the domestic commercial paper market, nearer in fact to 90 days. Investors which had been accustomed to time-deposits and primary CDs of maturities of three and six months may have changed their credit decision in opting to purchase a corporate or sovereign note but it did not necessarily imply a change in the desired maturity profile of their portfolio. Issuers, it must be remembered, even if they had a domestic commercial paper programme, were often entering the Euro-commercial paper market on an experimental basis and hence very few were prepared initially to make the necessary personnel adjustments and cost outlays to handle constant daily issuance. With an average programme size between $100 million and $200 million it was almost hardly worth the effort.

NUMBER AND SELECTION OF DEALERS

There is no hard and fast rule on the optimum number of dealers on a Euro-commercial paper programme. The market consensus to date suggests that for a programme up to $100 million in size two or three dealers are sufficient. Up to $200–250 million three dealers are usual whereas over that amount and up to $500 million four-dealer programmes are appropriate. Each dealer is implicitly expected to place between $50–125 million of the issuer's paper depending on the overall size of the programme. Sole dealership programmes are not very common and tend to be less than $100 million in size. Often they are programmes established on an experimental basis with a view to exploring a new market and the dealer tends to be a key relationship bank. The selection of dealers in general tends to be a mix of the issuer's relationship banks and those recognised as being particularly strong in Euro-commercial paper placement. The danger exists that a purely relationship-driven choice without regard to placement skills may cause the programme to underperform. To achieve the correct balance in the dealer group is a difficult task and not to be underestimated. Coverage of the investor base is a key criterion for issuers in selecting dealers and, although the nationality of the bank is not a good proxy for geography of placement, it is widely accepted as so. With the market still so young and banks' specific placement strengths a closely-guarded secret, issuers are at a disadvantage in being able to select dealers on placement record and ability. One of the best and increasingly used methods of selecting dealers is for new issuers to discuss with existing issuers their experience of the performance of particular dealers. This will be objective evidence.

Programmes with a large number of dealers, ie over five, need to be very carefully handled if they are to be truly successful. Unless there is a communality of objectives amongst issuer and dealers and a disciplined approach to yield and end investor placement, such programmes can seriously underperform. With dealers not committed to developing an investor base for the issuer's paper, the paper can become only loosely placed and then traded in the professional market at erratic yields relative to the paper of issuers of equivalent standing.

THE EXPORT DEVELOPMENT CORPORATION OF CANADA PROGRAMME

It took a major breakthrough to establish the Euro-commercial paper programme as an internationally acceptable borrowing structure as well as to demonstrate the benefits of constant daily offering of paper. This breakthrough came in May 1985 when the Export Development Corporation of Canada (EDC) established a programme totally new in both structure and concept. It started with two dealers, Credit Suisse First Boston Limited and Swiss Bank Corporation International Limited (with Union Bank of Switzerland Securities Limited joining six months later). It remains to this day the most successful Euro-commercial paper programme in terms of cost and it provided at an important moment in the market's development an enormous amount of impetus and publicity, causing more borrowers to consider the market as a serious alternative funding source. This is a curious phenomenon because the EDC programme is quite untypical of most Euro-commercial paper programmes and was founded on a fundamentally different principle.

Almost all Euro-commercial paper programmes are established with a view to the raising of finance at levels equally or more competitive than existing sources of short-term finance. Very few are established purely for purposes of diversification of fund sources or name-enhancement. The cheapest source of short-term US dollar finance for most creditworthy borrowers is the domestic commercial paper market and consequently Euro-commercial paper is most often compared to its US counterpart. EDC's fundamentally different approach in its programme was to attempt to raise funds tied to the yield on US Treasury bills, the lowest US dollar funding benchmark in the global market, i e the rate at which the US government funds itself rather than the domestic commercial paper market. As a government agency EDC's Euro-Treasury Notes are a charge on and payable out of the Consolidated Revenue Fund of Canada and thus EDC represents the sovereign risk of Canada. Its long-term debt enjoys the highest official rating, AAA/aaa, as does its short-term debt, A1+/P1. It is a highly-regarded borrower in the Euromarkets and hence well known to a large number of investors. EDC actually calls its programme, the 'Euro-Treasury Note' programme and, given its sovereign risk, it presents itself to Euro-investors as the first real US dollar-denominated alternative to the US Treasury bill.

The Euro-Treasury Notes are priced relative to T-bills rather than any bank liability benchmark such as LIBID or a Euro-CD rate. The notes are offered for maturities ranging from 7 to 364 days and, depending on the maturity, are priced on average between 10 and 25 basis points above the T-bill rate. In particular, the notes are primarily aimed at the Swiss market where retail investors and managed funds are large buyers of US Treasury bills, arguing that for a small increase in return Canadian sovereign risk can replace US sovereign risk. The programme is not restricted to the Swiss market but is available to investors all over the world, except for the US where it was feared the Euro-Treasury Notes might compete with its large commercial paper programme. Similarly, EDC does not permit its domestic commercial paper to be sold outside the US.

The methodology of the programme is the groundbreaking feature and the key to its success. EDC posts to the dealers by telex overnight from Canada a range of yields based on the North American market's close. Although the programme caters for all maturities between 7 and 364 days the range might look similar to this:

Maturity (months)	1	2	3	4	5	6	9	12
Issuing yield	5.70%	5.80%	5.80%	5.80%	5.85%	5.90%	6.00%	6.00%
Based on Treasury yield	5.19%	5.64%	5.71%	5.70%	5.84%	5.87%	5.97%	5.97%

These are firm yields at which the dealers have full authority to sell Euro-Treasury Notes. Dealers have discretion to sell notes to investors for broken periods and will choose the nearer, shorter-maturity posted yield but they will go to the next, longer-maturity yield if the broken period maturity shows only a few days' discrepancy. Therefore, if the investor wants a 45-day maturity, the 30-day rate would tend to be used; for 80 days the 90-day maturity would be selected. The amount that can be raised in each maturity is flexible and EDC tends to use the price mechanism to encourage and discourage sales in certain maturities, ie if it does not want six-month funds it will post a low yield. Because of the geographical distance and time zone EDC necessarily leaves some discretion to its dealers as to amounts to accept but if a very large amount was available in one maturity, a telephone call may have to be made to EDC. In essence, therefore, the dealers have almost complete freedom to offer paper to investors at a known price for any maturity between 7 and 364 days. The dealers act as agent in the programme and are not permitted to buy notes for their own account. This avoids the danger of position-taking and possible 'dumping' of paper at higher relative yields which might damage EDC's issuing yield over time. As sales are intended for end investors which hold to maturity, no active secondary market in Euro-Treasury Notes exists. The dealers will always make a bid-offer price to any investor wishing to sell before maturity and if the paper cannot be resold, EDC is prepared to repurchase the notes. This provides the liquidity support necessary to develop the investor base and is in fact very rarely used as the vast majority of investors hold to maturity. A separate sales commission is payable to the dealers by EDC as remuneration.

Further flexibility is provided by permitting a minimum investment amount as low as $10,000, rising in multiples of $1,000 with no maximum. Settlement would pose particular administrative problems if the programme were to use definitive notes and thus a different settlement procedure was required. No definitive notes are issued and the investor's rights are held in a global note each of which is held in the main office of each issuing and paying agent. Each investment is recorded on a book-entry basis and EDC, on maturity of each 'note', transfers its face value to the paying agent which is then responsible for repaying each investor.[2] The absence of definitive notes has not been an impediment to the programme and investors which normally prefer to hold definitive notes have been comfortable in the knowledge that the global note and book-entry system is managed by three of the world's strongest banks.

---

2 A detailed description of general settlement procedures is contained in chapter 6 below.

The success of the EDC programme has been outstanding and selected details of its results since 1 January 1986 demonstrate this.

1 Amount outstanding 30/6/86	$302 million
2 Average amount outstanding 1/1/86–30/6/86	$257 million

3 Average cost relative to T-bills (as % p a)

	1 month	3 months	6 months	9 months
T-bills plus	0.25	0.25	0.20	0.10

4 Average cost relative to LIBOR (as % p a)

	1 month	3 months	6 months	9 months
LIBOR minus	0.85	0.55	0.55	0.50
LIBID minus	0.73	0.42	0.42	0.37

5 Weighted average maturity (since 1/1/86):	60 days
6 Average issuance size:	$186,915

Source: EDC

In conclusion, the chief reasons for the success of the EDC programme are twofold: issuing methodology and price. The constant availability of paper is a boon to investor and dealer alike. Notes are available in size every business day for any maturity and, for the dealer, it solves one of the structural problems of the euronote market – security of supply at a known price. Price also is critical but price relativity rather than absolute rate. Euro-Treasury Notes are an alternative to T-bills and are consistently priced at a margin above T-bills rather than relative to a LIBID or LIBOR benchmark. Even when Eurodollar interest rates are significantly higher than T-bill rates the price relativities are maintained. At the times when the T-bill/LIBOR spread widens, EDC's holding of the T-bill margin on the Euro-Treasury Notes means that its margin under LIBOR also widens and traditional Euro-instrument investors are therefore much less likely to buy the notes. Investors which are regular buyers of T-bills are unaffected by the widening of the T-bill/LIBOR spread and their purchasing pattern of the Euro-Treasury Notes remains unchanged. On the whole most investors in EDC Euro-Treasury Notes have been attracted out of T-bills rather than Euro-instruments tied to LIBOR. A few other programmes followed – Nestlé, Mitsubishi Corporation, Fiat – all based on the same methodology though with minor modifications to suit issuer preferences.

EDC established certain themes and practices which came to characterise the Euro-commercial paper market – regular (if not constant) availability of paper and price control. In other words, the EDC programme was totally investor-driven, yet it was atypical in that it was retail-oriented and priced off a T-bill rather than a LIBOR benchmark.

The Euro-commercial paper programme accelerated in popularity throughout 1985 and established its ascendancy as the 'proper' method of issuing short-term debt obligations. Euronote issuance facilities began to decline and, although some major borrowers arranged such facilities, they sometimes included a Euro-commercial paper programme. For example, Broken Hill Proprietary Company Limited, the largest Australian company, arranged a $1,000 million facility comprising a euronote issuance facility of

$700 million and a separately documented Euro-commercial paper programme of $300 million. Some borrowers already using a tender panel recognised its inherent rigidities and sought to add more flexibility. This was best achieved through allowing all or certain of the tender panel members to make unsolicited bids and documentation was renegotiated to accommodate this. Unsolicited bids (called also 'direct bidding') in a tender panel operate in the same way as in a Euro-commercial paper programme described earlier in this chapter. Examples of this are the Unilever Capital Corporation $1,000 million facility and the Kingdom of Sweden's facility renegotiated and reduced to $2,000 million. The latter has experienced some success by adding direct bidding and at the time of writing has about $800 million of outstanding euronotes, $600 million by way of tender panel and $200 million through direct bidding. The cost via direct bidding has been maintained at around the same level as the results under tender panel bidding with some sales at 0.12% pa below LIBID.

Table 15

Euro-commercial paper programmes

VOLUME AND NUMBER BY TYPE OF ISSUER

	1985		1986 (until mid-July)	
	$m	No	$m	No
Corporate	7661	(52)	9610	(67)
Sovereign	3600	(22)	2554	(12)
Supranational	–	(–)	200	(1)
Bank	5950	(20)	14575	(51)
TOTAL	17211*	(94)	26939	(131)

* includes 9 amount unspecified/unlimited
\# includes 14 amount unspecified/unlimited

Source: IFR

Estimates of paper in issue by the end of 1985 tend to confirm a market of about $15–17 billion. The proportion of that market comprising Euro-commercial paper as opposed to euronotes found little consensus. At the time of writing there are no reliable statistics evidencing the split between Euro-commercial paper and euronotes for mid-1986. The view must be that with 131 programmes (an increase of 38 over December 1985) Euro-commercial paper now has the dominant share.

The Kingdom of Spain in June 1986 and Telefonica, the Spanish telecommunications company, arranged facilities in which certain of those banks providing a major underwriting commitment would be able to bid directly for euronotes, effectively becoming a dealer for the euronotes. A number of banks with euronote placement capabilities, but which were not underwriters in the facilities, would also be permitted to make direct bids. This highlighted some of the old infighting between commercial banks and investment banks which was perhaps now even more intense. One investment bank with a proven track-record in note placement might be selected as a dealer but another with an equally good note placement capability might not because its place would be taken by a commercial bank which may have made a precondition of its providing a significant commitment in the facility that it becomes a dealer. In this way the borrower risked diluting the performance potential of its euronotes by continuing to couple note placement with underwriting. This manner of selection stems partly from the fact that straightforward credit insurance was viewed as unremunerative and low-priority business. Partly also it was due to banks seeing the potential commission earnings in placing euronotes. Commercial banks insist often on the opportunity to place paper in return for the unattractive business of providing the credit back-stop. The argument becomes more pointed when credit pricing is so low. On a $10 million commitment in a facility where the underwriting fee is a mere 0.05% p a, a bank will earn $5,000 p a. For most banks this barely covers capital costs. It need only sell, for example, $20 million of notes at a commission of 0.025% p a in one year to make the same profit. The sales commissions are high-quality earnings as the sales process (unless a position is being taken) does not require the cost of capital to be applied against it. It is hardly surprising that banks moved so enthusiastically away from credit insurance towards note placement.

CENTRAL BANK REGULATION

It has been argued that continuous central bank pressure to have capital applied to bank underwriting commitments in euronote issuance facilities was a principal cause of the move into uncommitted issuance structures. The evidence does not really support this view and it is easy to overestimate the effect of central bank deliberations on this subject. The problem was only publicly recognised by bank regulators when the euronote market was in full flow. Somewhat alarmed at the huge increase in the volume of euronote issuance facilities in 1984, central banks rightly sought to ensure that banks were treating their commitments in a sensible and conservative manner. Clearly some were not. The standby euronote issuance facility was largely to blame. Since it was the stated intention of an issuer not to use the facility but to hold it as a back-up to an alternative source of funds, banks often felt that there was less risk involved and they looked upon the facility or underwriting fee as a non-capital item. In the small example above, one bank may have felt that a 0.05% p a underwriting fee was attractive business, another may not. The former is more likely to book more of this business than the latter, though the credit and capital risks are the same for both.

Consequently, banks could achieve their fee income budget by writing a lot of underwriting business in the *hope* that they would not be called upon to provide funds. They further argued that it required the borrower's alternative source of funds to dry up as well as its inability to sell euronotes under the standby facility before they would have to fund the euronotes and thus take them as a risk asset into their balance sheet. Hence, as they were two steps away from funding, this could not be seen as a full-risk commitment.

To a certain extent this was accepted by bank regulators as reasonable market-risk but as they were accustomed to look at credit risk it could not be entirely classified as market risk. If the borrower's creditworthiness deteriorated, then its alternative source of funds as well as its ability to sell euronotes could quickly disappear and the underwriting banks would have to fund, thereby taking an asset onto the balance sheet. They therefore began to apply weightings to euronote issuance facilities as a proportion of the risk of a straightforward loan advance. In April 1985 the Bank of England first established the precedent by setting a weighting of 0.5 in the risk/asset ratio compared to a weighting of 1.0 for a straightforward loan advance. Dutch regulators followed suit later in 1985 and the German and Japanese regulatory authorities were expected to adopt similar measures.

This neither slowed down the growth in facility volume nor increased pricing levels (as some banks were optimistically forecasting). Nor did it really force borrowers into uncommitted programmes. Market participants at the time were in favour of central bank guidelines as a means of raising pricing levels but competition was so fierce that the threat of such guidelines had no effect. Central banks regulated only those banks under their control, so that the Bank of England's measures applied to UK-incorporated banks. The London branch of a Swiss bank is regulated by the Swiss National Bank which, along with several other central banks, most notably the Federal Reserve, did not apply any specific public measures. The weakness of this approach to the problem was that it was not an internationally concerted approach. Competitive pressures being so strong, those banks whose regulators had applied measures still had to and did compete for business despite their disadvantage. At the time of writing it is anticipated that a co-ordinated approach by central banks under the aegis of the Bank for International Settlements in Basle to all off-balance sheet items, including underwriting commitments in euronote issuance facilities, will come to fruition.

The constant offering of paper and control over price that were the hallmarks of the EDC programme became those of a number of other programmes by major issuers. However, these programmes remain few in number, even today, and whilst the Euro-commercial paper market can look to its American antecedent for its inspiration and model most issuers do not use their programme as they would in the US. We have mentioned that EDC was atypical of the market since it was retail-oriented, priced off a T-bill benchmark and primarily Swiss-targetted. It required a Euro-commercial paper programme aimed at institutional and corporate investors, priced relative to investors' options in the Euromarkets and internationally targetted.

This was provided by the PepsiCo Inc programme[2] signed on 8 January 1986,

2 A copy of a note used in the PepsiCo programme is to be found on p 93 below. It can usefully be
   contrasted with the note from the Associates' programmes on p 21. The difference in text
   required to be on the face of each note demonstrates the changes in relevant legislation between
   1980 and 1986, and the legislative environment is fully analysed in chapter 7 below.

for which the dealers were Salomon Brothers International Limited, Swiss Bank Corporation International Limited and Union Bank of Switzerland (Securities) Limited. As a household name and a prime credit it was one of the first major US borrowers to arrange a programme and it demonstrated to other US companies which were large issuers in the domestic commercial paper market that there were potential benefits for them in the Euro-commercial paper market. It is a disciplined programme and was probably the first truly investor-led Euro-commercial paper programme in the market.

PepsiCo totally controls the yield at which its notes sell by posting rates each day for all maturities up to 183 days. The dealers are permitted to adjust rates without reference to PepsiCo if there is a significant shift in Eurodollar interest rates. The dealers act as agents and are not permitted to inventory paper nor to sell to other market professionals. This is stipulated out of a desire to sell only to genuine end-investors and to avoid possible yield-contamination by 'leakage' of paper to banks which do not have the same commitment as the dealers to end-investor placement. Once again, as in the EDC programme, a secure supply of paper is obtained and the dealers can offer it to their investors each day at a known price. This is of critical importance for building a diverse and substantial investor base – dealers will turn in the first instance to programmes where there is a secure source of supply in order to service their investor clients.

A number of other major borrowers with large domestic commercial paper programmes followed suit. Most notable was the British Petroleum Company plc in February 1986 which established a $500 million programme along similar lines to PepsiCo with daily posted rates and the willingness to issue reasonable amounts of paper in any maturity. This has become one of the largest investor-driven, corporate programmes in the market.

1986 has seen an acceleration in the growth of Euro-commercial paper programmes. Table 15 above shows that 94 individual programmes were established in 1985 and 131 in the first six months of 1986. There have been two principal areas where this growth is concentrated: US companies and banks.

NEW TYPES OF ISSUERS: US COMPANIES AND BANKS

In 1985 only 22 US issuers established Euro-commercial paper programmes whereas in the first six months of 1986, 39 did so. With its massive commercial paper market, the US is a natural source of creditworthy companies which might form a large sector of the Euro-commercial paper market. The companies are not only conversant with the operational procedures of such a market but are formally rated by the major rating agencies. US companies have had to be persuaded that the Euro-commercial paper market can offer an equivalent or cheaper borrowing cost than domestic sources of finance. The relative absence of US issuers in the early months attests to the doubt that the Euromarkets, being tied to the LIBID/LIBOR benchmarks, could be competitive with the domestic commercial paper market. This was more prejudice than fact and probably stemmed from the assumption that the historically wide differential between domestic commercial paper rates and LIBOR still prevailed. The facts do not support the assumption. The graphs in tables 18–22 below show the convergence of interest rates on certain US money market instruments compared to those on Eurodollar interest rates and instruments. In all cases the convergence of the graph lines is clear.

US issuers have also been attracted by the Euro-commercial paper market's investor preference for maturities longer than those available most competitively in the domestic commercial paper market. Historically 90-day and 180-day investments have been relatively standard in the Euromarkets compared to less than 30 days in the US. Whilst an increasing number of Euro-investors (especially the corporate investor) are shortening their average investment maturity, the differential still holds good. In the longest maturities (ie six months) the Euro-commercial paper market has been seen to offer substantially better cost and volume competitiveness compared to the domestic market.

The number of bank issuers rose from 20 in 1985 to 51 in the first half of 1986. Moreover, the average programme size for banks is $285 million twice that of corporates at $143 million. Just as with the euronote issuance facilities, banks tended to become a dominant factor in the new Euro-commercial paper market. The basic reason is that banks have large, constant funding needs and seem to be more willing to experiment with new markets and structures, especially with the strategic view of diversifying their funding sources. As banks tend also to be regular issuers (as opposed to corporates which can be relatively seasonal or cyclical in their funding needs), the volume of actual paper in the market is probably higher relative to the number of bank programmes. Since banks are active issuers, dealers have energetically sought this business since regular turnover is more profitable.

The question has been asked whether the Euro-commercial paper market risks becoming more a Euro-CD market because of the high number of bank issuers. Bank programmes vary as to whether they issue actual notes or certificates of deposit or both (in the Union Bank of Finland programme, for example, investors can choose whether to buy CDs or notes). Where they issue both it is vital that each type of instrument ranks equally with the other, lest a two-tier market develops. However, merely calling a bank programme Euro-commercial paper does not necessarily mean that it reaches an investor base or a cost-level that a corporate or sovereign programme may attain. A number of bank programmes, especially the very large ones, are really another way of accessing the CD markets. As this latter market tends to trade in 'runs' (ie a group of banks of similar creditworthiness are grouped together and a purchaser will obtain the same yield on the paper of any bank in that group) and hence can be a little 'anonymous', a specific Euro-commercial paper programme highlights the name of a particular bank and can give sales of its paper more impetus. This does not alter the fact that most often the paper is traded as in the CD market and it is difficult to rationalise how a bank's Euro-commercial paper notes can sell at yields below its regular CDs. The most successful bank programmes in terms of achieving relative cost benefits and opening up new investor sources are those for small or medium-sized European (or, particularly, non-US) banks which have little or no Latin American debt exposure and no asset concentration in depressed sectors such as energy and shipping.

Analysing bank issuers highlights a key trend identified in earlier chapters as a stimulus to the growth of a Euro-commercial paper market, the decline in creditworthiness of the bank sector. Not only has this caused investors to reconsider their investment options and caused them to buy corporate and sovereign paper, but it has engendered a spate of programmes for banks not associated with the huge problems facing other, mainly US, banks. Investors are comfortable with their risk and find their willingness to issue regularly or on demand highly convenient. We should not forget this key trend as it did not end with the Federal Reserve's action over Continental Illinois in 1984; if anything, the bank sector has further declined. The Latin American debt crisis still looms large and affects many large international banks. Continuing energy and agricultural problems have caused severe credit problems for certain US regional banks. Although capital requirements are higher and accounting procedures and disclosures are tougher, over 50 federally insured banks failed in the first six months of 1986. There were 120 failures in 1985. The Federal Deposit Insurance Corporation is estimated to have over 1,300 banks on its 'problem list' compared with 200 five years ago. The rapid deterioration of BankAmerica, formerly the largest bank in the world and now downgraded from AAA to BBB has been a surprising and almost symbolic occurrence. Its effect has been to reinforce the investor's view of this trend which first began three or four years previously when the earliest signs of the decline in bank creditworthiness became evident. Dealers have noticed in the twelve months to mid-1986 a dramatic increase in the number of corporate and institutional investors which have entered the Euro-commercial paper market for purposes not only of yield enhancement but of risk diversification.

Table 16

Bank programmes by domicile of issuer

	1985	1986*
W Europe	14	27
US	3	10
Australia	2	3
Japan	1	9
Other	0	2
	20	51

* until mid-July

Source: IFR

THE CONVERGENCE OF DOMESTIC AND EURODOLLAR INTEREST RATES

There are a number of causes contributing to the convergence of domestic and Eurodollar interest rates. One of the main causes occurred in 1980 when the

Monetary Control Act in the US effected a reduction in banks' reserve requirements from 8% to 3% by 1984. As domestic CDs tended to rise in yield, this led to a substantial realignment of the differential between domestic CDs and Euro-CDs (the latter not being subject to such reserve requirements). Tables 18 and 19 illustrate this. Over time that differential has fallen to an approximate average of only two or three basis points. The same legislation led to eventual de-control of some aspects of the US financial system, notably allowing commercial banks to move their deposit rates to compete for retail funds. As US commercial banks increasingly obtained their liabilities from this source, the average volume of CDs bought by money market funds dropped significantly from over $35 billion at the end of 1982 to under $14 billion by the end of 1985. A concomitant of this fall was the increase in the proportion of domestic commercial paper held by such funds – rising from $50 billion in 1982 to almost $90 billion in 1985. This tracks a rise in the overall outstandings of domestic commercial paper from $160 million to $290 million during this period. Table 22 amply demonstrates this fact as well as the overall reduction in CD volume.

With the convergence of domestic and Eurodollar interest rates the traditional cost competitiveness of the domestic commercial paper market is eroded and becomes suspect. Care must be taken when comparing the relative cost of issuing in the domestic and Euro-commercial paper markets. Domestic rates are quoted on a discount basis and so must be converted to the money-market yield which the Euro-commercial paper market uses. In addition it is necessary to clarify what other cost elements are being included in the comparison.

Dealer commissions are standard in the US market (except, of course, for direct issuers) and are thus an integral cost element. They are *not* standard in the Euro-commercial paper market – some issuers pay an explicit commission, some issue on a net price basis. Some borrowers include the cost of the back-up credit lines required to be able to issue in the domestic market. At the present time inclusion of the back-up credit lines would tend to make the cost of Euro-commercial paper more advantageous as commitment/facility fees in the Euromarkets are generally well below those in the US credit markets. Without the inclusion of back-up credit lines the incidence of Euro-commercial paper being more competitive than domestic commercial paper is increasingly frequent.

Table 17

Differential between LIBOR and US commercial paper rates (% p a)

	1981	1982	1983	1984	1985	1986*
1 month	0.73	0.79	0.44	0.29	0.14	0.18
3 month	0.78	0.82	0.48	0.35	0.18	0.15

* until June

Source: SBCI

Taking all this against a background of generally falling interest rates, the differential between Euro-rates and domestic commercial paper has narrowed significantly during the last two to three years. Table 20 shows that the differential between one-month LIBOR and one-month domestic commercial paper has fallen from 0.79% p a to 0.18% p a for the first six months of 1986. To evaluate this relative to LIBID 0.125% p a should be deducted, being the usual differential between LIBOR and LIBID. The three-month differential reduction has been even more impressive, from 0.82% p a to 0.15% p a.

RATINGS

Formal short-term debt ratings by the professional rating agencies have long been a feature of the domestic commercial paper market. They have in the last twelve months become increasingly prevalent in the Euro-commercial paper market. The two rating agencies which have decided to establish offices in London in order to rate Euro-commercial paper are Standard and Poor's and Moody's Investors Service Inc and both agencies dominate the domestic US rating scene. Both have opted to use their existing US symbols to indicate the relative repayment ability of rated issuers. For Moody's the symbols are Prime-1, Prime-2, Prime-3 and Not Prime; the first three designating, respectively, a superior, strong or acceptable ability for repayment of short-term debt obligations. The Not Prime designation means that the issuer does not fall in any of the first three grades and is therefore below investment grade. Standard and Poor's uses the symbols A1+, A1, A2, A3, B, C and D. An A1+ rating denotes an overwhelming degree of safety and A1 denotes a very strong degree of safety. A2 is designated 'strong' and A3 'satisfactory regarding timely payment of obligations'. The B and C rating denote, respectively, 'adequate' and 'doubtful capacity for timely payment'. The D rating indicates that the issue is either in default or expected to be so on maturity.

The number of rated Euro-commercial paper programmes has increased significantly with the entry of more US issuers into the market. European borrowers with experience of ratings either through a long-term debt issue or a domestic commercial paper programme are now more inclined to use ratings on their Euro-commercial paper. There still, however, remains a prejudice against ratings amongst non-US borrowers, principally because they regard the rating process as expensive in both management time and money. The rating agencies are at pains to explain precisely the time and expense involved in the rating process in order to allay that prejudice. Issuers have felt it more necessary to rate their Euro-commercial paper because of the rise of the non-bank investor which does not have the time or expertise to undertake a credit analysis of the issuer. The non-bank investor typically seeks internal management or board approval to invest in paper that is only rated A1+, A1 or P1, thereby taking the rating as a proxy for credit quality. An issuer, therefore, which decides not to rate its paper can risk automatically excluding itself from the approved investment list of many investors. One of the unfortunate 'side-effects' of this convenient approach is investors' rejection of A2 or P2 paper which can be a good and relatively high-yielding short-term credit risk. Only

Table 18

Historical Interest Rate Comparison*

30-Day Maturity

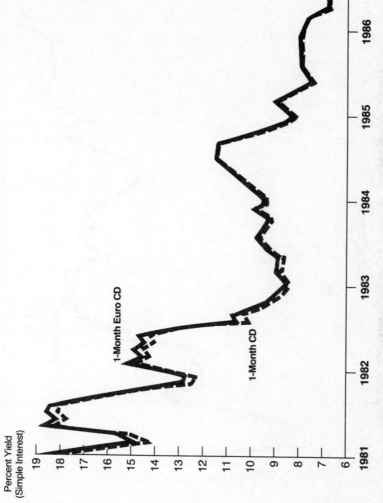

Percent Yield
(Simple Interest)

1-Month Euro CD

1-Month CD

* All yields calculated on a simple-interest basis.

Source: Goldman Sachs Money Markets Inc.

Table 19   **Historical Interest Rate Comparison***

90-Day Maturity

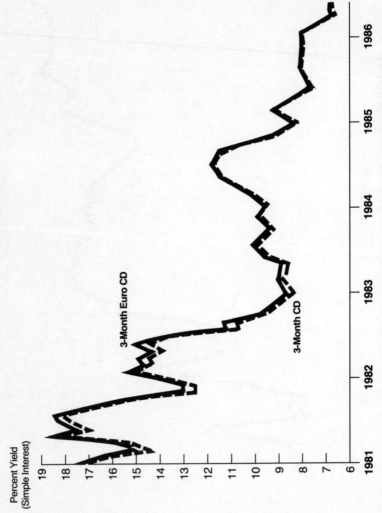

Percent Yield
(Simple Interest)

3-Month Euro CD

3-Month CD

1981   1982   1983   1984   1985   1986

* All yields calculated on a simple-interest basis.

Source: Goldman Sachs Money Markets Inc.

Table 20

Historical Interest Rate Comparison *

30-Day Maturity

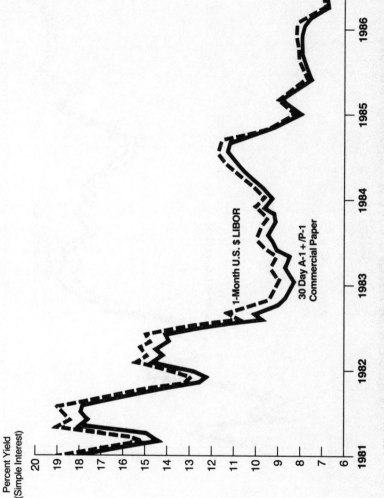

Percent Yield
(Simple Interest)

1-Month U.S. $ LIBOR

30 Day A-1 + /P-1
Commercial Paper

* All yields calculated on a simple-interest basis.

Source: Goldman Sachs Money Markets Inc.

Table 21

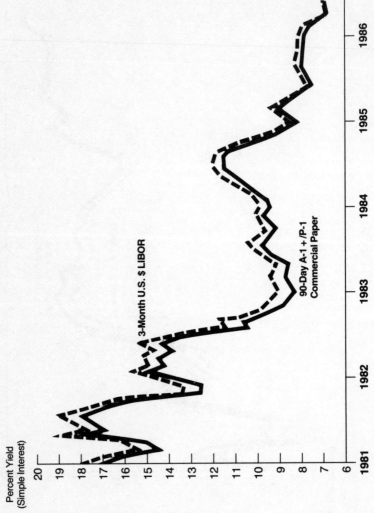

Historical Interest Rate Comparison*
90-Day Maturity

Percent Yield
(Simple Interest)

3-Month U.S. $ LIBOR

90-Day A-1 + /P-1
Commercial Paper

20
19
18
17
16
15
14
13
12
11
10
9
8
7
6

1981   1982   1983   1984   1985   1986

* All yields calculated on a simple-interest basis.

Source: Goldman Sachs Money Markets Inc.

Table 22

U.S. Money Market Instruments Outstanding

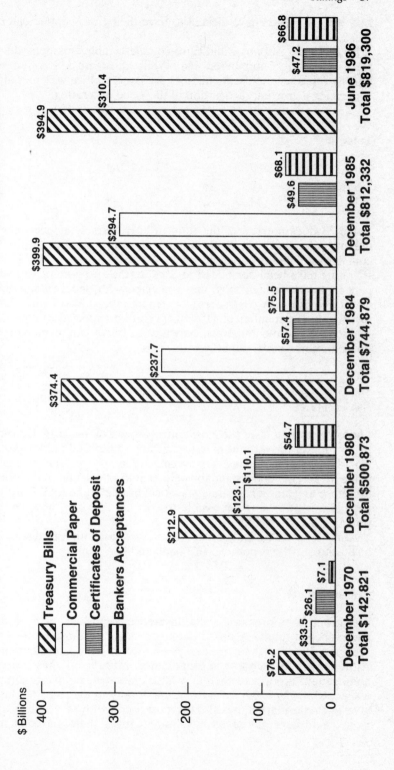

$ Billions

Legend:
- Treasury Bills
- Commercial Paper
- Certificates of Deposit
- Bankers Acceptances

December 1970
Total $142,821
- $76.2
- $33.5
- $26.1
- $7.1

December 1980
Total $500,873
- $212.9
- $123.1
- $110.1
- $54.7

December 1984
Total $744,879
- $374.4
- $237.7
- $57.4
- $75.5

December 1985
Total $812,332
- $399.9
- $294.7
- $49.6
- $68.1

June 1986
Total $819,300
- $394.9
- $310.4
- $47.2
- $66.8

two non-US issuers have elected to have their Euro-commercial paper rated A2P2.

By July 1986 euronotes and Euro-commercial paper issuers which had been rated by Moody's numbered 118. Whilst most are US issuers which were already rated, an increasing number are issuers which were not already rated evidencing a growing recognition of the value of a rating.

Table 23

	P1	*P2*	*P3*	*NP*
US issuers	49	21	1	1
Non-US issuers	44	2	–	–

Table 23 does not reflect the total of borrowers actually issuing paper but merely those borrowers with either a euronote issuance facility or a Euro-commercial paper programme which Moody's has rated. 21 US issuers with a P2 rating have been persuaded to come to the euronote or Euro-commercial paper market (though most are connected with undrawn standby facilities) whilst only two non-US issuers have entered the market with a P2 rating. The increase in the number of US issuers can be expected to continue as more realise that Euro-commercial paper can offer a complementary market to domestic commercial paper.

INVESTORS

Obviously this is one of the most critical aspects of the entire Euro-commercial paper market for without investors willing to buy and hold paper the market would be little more than a narrow circle of inter-professional traders. Dealers in the market are understandably reluctant to give details of their investors and therefore any kind of accurate statistical profile of the total Euro-commercial paper investor base is impossible to compile. We can, however, review the principal investor sectors.

It will be useful to categorise the investor base into four distinct groups: (i) institutional, (ii) corporates, (iii) bank and (iv) retail.

(i) Institutional

This group comprises, inter alia, insurance companies, pension funds, trusts and managed funds. A broad definition might be those entities for which a substantial part of their business is the professional management of money. Although grouped under the generic title 'institutional' these are not a purely homogenous group and each may have quite distinct investment preferences and practices. Not only does this group represent the largest volume of funds invested in the market, it is also the most consistently invested. As professional money managers they generally require to invest their funds on a regular basis and contend with cyclicality of funds flows to a much lesser extent than corporate investors. The institutional investor sector, by its very size, is and will continue to be, the mainstay of the Euro-commercial paper market. The average sales ticket size tends to be larger than with the other investor groups. Dealers wishing to establish themselves in the market as a whole must have good institutional market coverage since it provides them with the high volume of turnover so necessary for Euro-commercial paper to be an economically viable business.

(ii) Corporates

The growing interest and activity by the corporate investor has been one of the major successes of the Euro-commercial paper market and represents a key difference from the earlier programmes. The corporate differs markedly from the institutional investor in that it tends to have a cyclical cash flow and thus may not be a regular investor. Given seasonal cash flows, some are investors for one half of the year and issuers for the other half. Some dealers, as a result, tend not to focus seriously on this group because it cannot offer sufficient turnover volume to make economic sense.

A further complication is that corporate investor liquidity in the Euromarkets tends not to be in US dollars but in the corporate's local currency and hence an additional step is required in the sales process. The dealer must swap the US dollar note into the currency of the corporate investor's liquidity on a fully-hedged basis so that the all-in cost of this option can be compared to alternative instruments in that currency. A numerical example of this is given below. The corporate investor group is a fast growing sector as treasurers seek both to diversify investment risk and to increase returns.

(iii) Retail

In the strict European sense, 'retail' means the private individual. The term can be used to mean non-financial institutions or notes held until maturity and care must be taken in defining what is meant by 'retail' in a particular context. As yet in the Euro-commercial paper market the retail investor base has been only slightly exploited. The EDC programme (see above) and the others of its type that followed have been the only ones to tap this market and this has been largely restricted to Switzerland.

Every major European country offers a potentially enormous retail market dominated in its own currency. In almost all cases those markets are surrounded by regulations of byzantine complexity prohibiting straightforward access by issuers and tax-effective exploitation by investors. To be effective in retail markets an issuer really must be prepared to offer paper constantly and in small denominations. Furthermore, unless the issuer requires that currency, it will have to convert into its own required borrowing currency. Operationally, therefore, the retail markets present problems of administration and management which, even assuming the regulatory and tax problems can be overcome, may outweigh any cost benefits. Nevertheless, individual retail markets present an alluring though complex prospect.

(iv) Banks

In the early Euro-commercial paper programmes and for many euronote issuance facilities banks represented the largest investor group. When notes could be sold at a positive margin above LIBOR, commercial banks were always a logical investor. This is because they consider LIBOR as a benchmark for their cost of funds and could match-fund the asset thereby locking in a margin. In many cases this exercise is tantamount to putting an asset on the commercial loan book.

With the enormous increase in the institutional and corporate investor sectors whose benchmark investment return could be taken as LIBID euronotes and Euro-commercial paper began to sell regularly below LIBOR, even for medium-risk credits. This clearly meant that banks could not buy such paper as it would cause them either to make a loss (if their funding cost really was LIBOR) or to set a market precedent for lower overall yields. Banks are a major investor today in the medium-to-low credit range where paper is offered at a margin above LIBOR.

However, a sea-change has come about over the last twelve months to mid-1986 in the wake of the continuing deterioration of certain areas of the commercial bank sector. Investors continue to be uncertain and thus diversify more out of bank instruments into Euro-commercial paper. But the biggest lenders to banks are banks themselves through the interbank market and it is clear that some are buying corporate and sovereign Euro-commercial paper as a substitute for bank CDs. Not only, in some cases, is a better yield obtainable, but the purchasing bank can improve its risk with little loss of liquidity. As dealers commit to support all their programmes, the purchasing bank knows it can enjoy excellent liquidity support in case of need even if it is somewhat less than that provided by the multiple market-makers of the CD market.

For investors Euro-commercial paper represents only one of several alternative investment media available. The dealer offering paper to investors has to be aware of what those alternatives are and gauge whether the risk, yield and maturity elements of Euro-commercial paper will be persuasive enough for the investor to buy. Typically an investor in the Eurodollar market might be able to select from a range of investment instruments: bank CDs, time-deposits, Treasury bills, floating-rate notes. This is a relatively straightforward decision and whilst risk, yield and maturity will be the key considerations, the investor will be concerned also with liquidity and ease of settlement. Euro-commercial paper compares favourably on all counts with competing instruments. In terms of risk there is now a wide range of programmes available offering all qualities of issuer. No one investment medium today can really offer the breadth of risk quality, yield and liquidity of the Euro-commercial paper market. CDs and time-deposits are exclusively bank risk media whilst the floating-rate note market has virtually no corporate risk to offer, being dominated by bank and sovereign issuers. Furthermore the floating-rate note is a long-term instrument and needs to be offered by a dealer on a repurchase basis (called a 'repo') to make it directly comparable with Euro-commercial paper; this adds a further element of dealer risk which takes the instrument back into the bank risk sector. As we have seen, the maturity range and flexibility offered by many Euro-commercial paper programmes can be better than the CD market and probably all other instruments. Liquidity is offered by all legitimate dealers in the market and is today perfectly adequate for most investors' purposes. Settlement is also straightforward and, except for a time-deposit, must represent one of the simplest procedures.

The pricing of Euro-commercial paper therefore takes place with regard to the cost of alternative Eurodollar investment instruments. For the investor whose liquidity is in a currency other than US dollars the dealer must follow the same principle: what is the cost of alternative investments in that currency? The dealer must be able to offer a US dollar note fully hedged into the investor's currency at a yield above those alternatives. The dealer must have a foreign exchange capability in order to be able to offer the investor an asset for which the investor simply pays in its local currency and on maturity receives repayment in its local currency. (In rare cases, an investor might purchase the US dollar note and effect the foreign exchange hedge itself but most consider this excessively labour-intensive and not worth any higher return achievable.) This is a large and growing feature of the Euro-commercial paper market and involves the dealer in much more effort than a simple sale to US dollar-based investors. The average transaction time for a fully hedged sale is probably three or four times longer than for a US dollar sale. It is worth looking at an example of how this would work.

Example 8

A Swiss investor has SFr 9,000,000 which it is prepared to invest for six months and is approached by a bank with the following securities:

Issuer:	Frito-Lay Inc
Guarantor:	PepsiCo Inc
Amount:	US$ 5,000,000
Coupon:	None (i e discount note)
Trade date:	19 May 1986
Value date:	21 May 1986
Maturity date:	20 November 1986

The investor is able to place a deposit with its bank at a rate of 4.125% p a. The dealer proposes that by purchasing the Frito-Lay note at a yield of 6.906% p a and fully hedging it into Swiss Francs, the investor could obtain a return of 4.25% p a.

The procedure would be as follows: the purchase consideration of the Frito-Lay notes at a 6.906% p a yield is

$$\frac{5,000,000}{1 + \left(\dfrac{6.906 \times 183}{36000}\right)}$$

= \$4,830,425.50

On the 19 May 1986 for value 21 May 1986 the dealer buys SFr 8,887,982.92 from the investor against US dollars at a spot rate of 1.8400. This is equivalent to $4,830,425.50, the purchase price of the securities. The dealer uses this amount of US dollars to purchase the Frito-Lay notes which are held in safe-custody on the investor's behalf in the dealer's securities account in one of the clearing systems. Alternatively, the investor may wish the securities to be transferred elsewhere to its order.

At the same time (ie 19 May 1986) for value 20 November 1986, the dealer buys the proceeds of the maturing notes (as they are discount notes, this amount will be $5,000,000) from the investor against Swiss Francs at a rate of 1.8160. This produces SFr 9,080,000.

On 20 November 1986 this Swiss Franc amount is repaid by the dealer to the investor and this provides a return of 4.25% pa, a ⅛% pa higher return than the investor's alternative investment option.

To check this yield:

$$\frac{(9,080,000 - 8,887,982.50)}{8,887,982.50} \times \frac{36,000}{183}$$

$$= 4.25\%$$

This has a drawback for the investor in that it is not able to invest an even SFr 9,000,000 but has to manage an awkward amount of cash (ie SFr 8,887,982.50). This is obviously because of the fluctuating foreign exchange rate but also because the underlying notes are limited to $500,000 denominations. With a global note where increments of $10,000 are available, providing the issuer is willing to issue a slightly larger US dollar amount, a Swiss Franc amount closer to the actual SFr 9,000,000 could be achieved. In this case a US dollar amount of $5,060,000 would have used SFr 8,994,638.71 of the investor's investible amount.

An example of a Euro-commercial paper note

PROMISSORY NOTE

(incorporated under the laws of the State of Delaware)

unconditionally guaranteed by

(incorporated under the laws of the State of Delaware)

No. 0 0000

Issue Date.....................................19......

Maturity Date...............................19......

....

For value received, Frito-Lay, Inc. (the "Issuer") promises to pay to the bearer on the above-mentioned Maturity Date the sum of

at and upon presentation and surrender of this Note to The Chase Manhattan Bank, N.A., London Branch, Woolgate House, Coleman Street, London EC2P 2HD (the "Agent"), such payment to be made by check mailed to an address outside the United States (as defined below) or, at the option of the bearer, by wire transfer to a bank account located outside the United States, in accordance with the Agency Agreement by and among the Issuer, Pepsico, Inc. and the Agent, dated January 7, 1986, copies of which are available at the offices of the Agent.

The obligations of the Issuer in respect of this Note are guaranteed by PepsiCo, Inc. (the "Guarantor"), pursuant to the terms of a Guarantee (the "Guarantee"). Copies of the Guarantee are available at the offices of the Agent.

This Note is issued subject to and with the benefit of the terms endorsed on the reverse hereof.

This Note shall not be validly issued unless authenticated by the Agent.

This Note and the Guarantee are governed by, and shall be construed in accordance with, the laws of the State of New York.

IN WITNESS WHEREOF the Issuer has caused this Note to be duly signed in facsimile on its behalf.

Certificate of authentication

THE CHASE MANHATTAN BANK, N.A., LONDON BRANCH   **FRITO-LAY, INC.**

By: ....   By: ....
(Authorized Signatory)   (Authorized Signatory)

By: ....   By: ....
(Authorized Signatory)   (Authorized Signatory)

THIS NOTE HAS NOT BEEN AND WILL NOT BE REGISTERED UNDER THE SECURITIES ACT OF 1933, AS AMENDED, OF THE UNITED STATES OR THE SECURITIES LAWS OF ANY STATE OR OTHER POLITICAL SUBDIVISION OF THE UNITED STATES AND MAY NOT BE OFFERED, SOLD, RESOLD OR DELIVERED DIRECTLY OR INDIRECTLY, IN THE UNITED STATES OR TO OR FOR THE ACCOUNT OF ANY UNITED STATES PERSON. "UNITED STATES" MEANS THE UNITED STATES OF AMERICA, ITS TERRITORIES AND POSSESSIONS AND ALL AREAS SUBJECT TO ITS JURISDICTION, AND "UNITED STATES PERSON" MEANS ANY PERSON WHO IS A CITIZEN, NATIONAL OR RESIDENT OF THE UNITED STATES, ANY CORPORATION, PARTNERSHIP OR OTHER ENTITY CREATED OR ORGANIZED IN OR UNDER THE LAWS OF THE UNITED STATES OR ANY POLITICAL SUBDIVISION THEREOF, OR ANY ESTATE OR TRUST THAT IS SUBJECT TO UNITED STATES FEDERAL INCOME TAXATION REGARDLESS OF THE SOURCE OF ITS INCOME.

BY ACCEPTING THIS NOTE, THE HOLDER HEREOF REPRESENTS, WARRANTS AND AGREES (i) THAT IT IS NOT A UNITED STATES PERSON AND THAT IT IS NOT ACTING FOR OR ON BEHALF OF ANY UNITED STATES PERSON AND (ii) THAT IT IS HAS NOT OFFERED, SOLD, RESOLD OR DELIVERED, AND WILL NOT OFFER, SELL, RESELL OR DELIVER, THIS NOTE, DIRECTLY OR INDIRECTLY, IN THE UNITED STATES OR TO OR FOR THE ACCOUNT OF ANY UNITED STATES PERSON.

CHAPTER 6

Issuing, paying and clearing euronotes and Euro-commercial paper

We have in the past chapters discussed the purchase and sale of notes under euronote issuance facilities and Euro-commercial paper. We have not touched upon an indispensable feature of that process of purchase and sale, the actual issuing of the note, its delivery to and from investors and its payment upon maturity. This is commonly termed as 'settlement'.

This chapter deals with two operational aspects of the Euro-commercial paper market:

(i) issuing and paying agency; and
(ii) clearing.

Both these functions are often taken for granted. However, they are essential, if mechanical, aspects of every euronote issuance facility and Euro-commercial paper programme. The efficiency with which these functions are carried out, and the methods employed, can have a significant impact on the overall viability of a facility or programme.

As we shall see later in this chapter, both functions are characterised at present by fierce competition between the providers of these services and a steady process of innovation has been stimulated not only by this competition, but also by the specific requirements of participants within the developing Euro-commercial paper market.

ISSUING AND PAYING AGENCY

As the term suggests, this consists of two activities.

(i) Issuing agency

This involves the issuing of the notes into the market on behalf of the issuer. The issuing agent will undertake the following functions and responsibilities:

– it will hold blank stocks of notes on behalf of the issuer. These notes will normally have been pre-signed ('executed') with a facsimile authorised signature of the issuer;
– when instructions are received to issue notes, either from the dealer(s) or the issuer direct, it will complete the appropriate number of blank notes with details such as issue date, maturity date, and denomination (if this is not pre-printed) and then sign the notes. The last process of signing is called

authentication and thus there are two separate sets of signatures on each note – those of the issuer and the issuing agent. When this has been done, the notes are live instruments and ready for delivery;

– it will deliver the completed notes to the initial purchaser or to the purchaser's order.[1] This initial purchaser may be one of the programme dealers or an investor;
– it will receive payment from the initial purchaser and make payment, on behalf of the purchaser, to the issuer.

In some cases, the issuing agent may be instructed to make delivery of the note without handling the payments. This is called a 'free delivery'. 'Free' in this case, of course, means simply that payment is handled as a separate matter and not tied to the delivery process. The purchaser makes payment to the issuer independently of delivery of the notes. This can be a risky process for both parties. In the majority of cases the issuing agent is instructed to make the delivery versus payment. This is much safer than free delivery. The details of how this is done, and the risks of free delivery and delivery versus payment, are discussed later in this chapter.

As the note is a bearer negotiable instrument, transfer from seller to purchaser is completed when the security is delivered. 'Delivery', of course suggests a physical movement of the notes. This does happen in many cases, but increasingly, through the use of clearing systems, the physical delivery of notes is being eliminated. In such cases, delivery of the note is effected by book-entry transfer from the account of the seller to the account of the buyer. The underlying notes do not physically move, but remain untouched in the clearing system's vaults. This process is reviewed in more detail later.

(ii) Paying agency

Paying agency involves the payment of holders of notes at maturity on behalf of the issuer. The paying agent will be responsible for:

– receiving notes from holders at maturity. The holders, or a custodian acting on their behalf, are said to 'present' their notes for payment;
– making payments to the presenters of notes or to their order;
– receiving payment from the issuer in respect of redemption of the notes;
– cancelling and destroying (or returning to the issuer) matured notes.

The paying agent needs to be familiar with the tax environment in which it operates. Under certain circumstances, it will need to withhold tax from the payments. The paying agent also needs to operate in such a way that it does not become exposed to unacceptable risk. It is, after all, transferring large sums of money and, as we shall see later, it may incur a significant intra-day exposure to the issuer.

The two activities – issuing agency and paying agency – are thus logically separate and can be (indeed sometimes are) performed by different entities. It is, however, more usual and practical for them both to be executed by the same entity.

1In London 'delivery' of instruments at issue is effected by making the notes available for collection by the purchaser (or its agent) at the issuing agent's window.

It is reasonable to question whether a separate issuing and paying agent is needed. In theory, the issuer does not need either agent since it could perform all the functions in issuing and paying the notes itself. However, it will be apparent from the earlier description of activities that this is something most issuers will find uneconomic and impractical. In order to carry out the issuing and paying functions, the minimum requirement would be:

- an office in the City of London. A City presence is needed to cope with physical delivery of notes to and from market participants. Nearly all investors will be holding their notes with banks or with London depositories located in the City for the major clearing systems. Most corporate and sovereign issuers will not have such an office;
- secure premises, where completed notes worth hundreds of millions of dollars, plus blank notes worth potentially billions of dollars, will need to be stored and handled. Professional issuing and paying agents will have high-security vaults for this purpose. Most corporate issuers (and indeed many banks) would not have suitable facilities;
- the means of physical delivery. This requires messengers and, of course, adequate insurance. The need for physical delivery is steadily being eliminated, but the means must nevertheless be available;
- the necessary expertise in effecting delivery versus payment;
- expertise in relevant withholding tax law.

It is therefore not surprising that virtually all issuers appoint an issuing and paying agent to handle these functions. The only real exceptions arise where an issuer is a bank which itself has an issuing and paying agency capability. In this case it may well carry out the functions for itself. Even so, a specialised unit within the organisation will still be involved.

The issuer makes the choice of issuing and paying agent. In making its decision, it may well consult its dealers for their advice and suggestions, bearing in mind their experience in working with agents on other programmes.

It may also wish to consult its colleagues in other organisations, who may already have set up a programme. Many agents are able to provide the basic issuing and paying agency services but the following criteria are relevant in selecting an agent:

(i)   does the agent have direct access to a major clearing system which handles short-term notes and/or CDs?

(ii)   can the agent provide same day settlement and if so, what is the deadline for receipt of instructions?

(iii)   does the agent have a good track record?

(iv)   can the agent also handle the issuing of commercial paper denominated in sterling, ECU or other currencies (which may be an option the issuer will require in the future)?

(v)   does the agent have the capacity to handle a large volume of note issuance at short notice late in the day?

(vi)   is the agent comfortable with handling very short maturity paper, including overnight?

(vii) does the agent have expertise in complying with various withholding tax rules?

(viii) is the agent committed to the service as an important business area and will resources be devoted to future product enhancement and innovation?

(ix) can the agent handle the type of note programme (conventional definitives, global notes, or universal notes) most suitable for the issuer?

CLEARING

This term is loosely used to cover a number of separate functions and processes. Clearing in its widest sense consists of:

(i) holding the notes on behalf of investors. This is referred to as the safekeeping or custodian function. It is logically separate from the remainder of the clearing process and may be carried out by a separate entity;

(ii) effecting the delivery of securities from the buyer to the seller, by physical delivery or by book-entry transfer. This is the essence of the clearing function;

(iii) arranging the associated transfer of funds from buyer to seller. This is referred to as *settlement*.

There are three situations in which a clearing agent will be involved in a transaction:

(i) where both buyer and seller are participants in the agent's clearing system;

(ii) where only the buyer is a participant, i e it is buying from an entity outside the clearing system;

(iii) where only the seller is a participant, i e it is selling to an entity outside the clearing system.

Where both buyer and seller of the note are participants in the same clearing system, the clearing system will 'match' the instructions received from each party to ensure consistency and accuracy. In cases (ii) and (iii) the clearing system can only rely on instructions from one party. Instructions must be effected by secure means. The most frequent methods used are tested telex and electronic communication from the customer's terminal to the clearing system. Other methods include SWIFT and messenger delivery of written instructions. Electronic communications is steadily becoming the norm.

Where both buyer and seller are holding their securities with the clearing system, delivery of the securities will be by book-entry transfer. If the seller is selling to a party outside the system, the clearing system (or its depository) will physically deliver the securities, preferably against an irrevocable undertaking of payment, to the purchaser's designated bank. If the purchaser is buying from a party outside the system, the securities will be delivered to the system's depository which will give a receipt.

The clearing system will settle the total payments of each participant on a net basis at the end of the day. It also will pay outside sellers and receive funds from outside buyers on behalf of its participants. Payments in US dollars are settled via either the CHIPS or Fed Wire system.

Why is a clearing agent needed? As with issuing and paying, a clearing system is not essential because buyers and sellers of securities could, in theory, perform all the necessary functions themselves. Indeed, some banks handle the clearing of their own short-term instruments, whether notes or CDs. However, there are also some compelling benefits to using a centralised clearing system. These can be summarised as:

- to the extent that buyer and seller are participants in the same clearing system, a reduction in the need for physical delivery, thus minimising cost, risk and delay in settling transactions;
- where physical delivery is required, the availability of messenger staff to effect delivery;
- where the securities are being received from an outside seller, the presence of trained staff and sophisticated devices to check and guard against counterfeit and/or fraudulently altered securities;
- secure vaults;
- the ability for participants to settle on a net basis with the clearing system instead of on an individual basis with each counterparty;
- the provision of comprehensive and timely accounting information to participants.

Table 24

Issuing and paying agency

TYPICAL TIMETABLE OF EVENTS AT ISSUING AND MATURITY

Issue date	Method	Deadline
IPA notified of details of new issue (amount, maturity, price, delivery)	Electronic link or Telex	4.00 pm (London time)
IPA completes and authenticates notes	Computer printer	Close of business (London)
IPA issues notes into dealer's custody account	Book entry	
IPA credits issuer's account, debits dealer's account	Book entry	
IPA pays same-day value funds to issuer's bank in US, according to standing instructions	CHIPS	Close of business (New York)
Dealer settles with IPA on a net basis	CHIPS	
Next business day		
IPA informs issuer of serial numbers, etc of notes issued	Electronic link or mail	

Maturity date	Method	Deadline
Issuer pays funds to IPA	CHIPS	10.00 am (New York time)
IPA pays funds to investors	CHIPS	} Close of business (London)
IPA cancels and destroys paid notes	Manual	

Next business day

IPA informs issuer of notes paid and notes outstanding	Electronic link or mail	

This timetable assumes that *physical* delivery of notes is not required – if it is, then the deadline for instructions would be 13.00 on issue date.

IPA = Issuing and Paying Agent
CHIPS = Clearing House Inter-Bank Payments System

ISSUANCE OF NOTES: DEFINITIVES, GLOBAL OR UNIVERSAL?

(i) Conventional definitive notes

Individual promissory notes are issued to investors under a programme in security-printed form. Features of security printing include special quality paper, the intaglio printing process, watermarking, fluorescent colouring and latent image. Definitives currently account for 70% of market transactions by volume. The conventional approach to Euro-commercial paper issuance is the completion and authentication of individual security-printed notes. For most issues, the cost of this is acceptably low. For example, the all-in cost of issuing a $500,000 denomination, three-month maturity note, including security-printing costs and issuing agent's fees, is less than one basis point (0.01%) per annum. However, for low denominations (say below $50,000) or short maturities (say less than one month) the cost of issuing conventional notes can become a significant element of the all-in cost of funds to the issuer.

(ii) Global notes

A single global note is issued for each drawdown under a programme and is held by a depository for a clearing system. The ownership of individual investors is then recorded on the books of the clearing system and no separate definitives are issued. Global notes were introduced in this market towards the middle of 1985. The global note was developed in an attempt to provide a lower-cost service to the issuer in such circumstances. Supposedly, the replacement of physical notes by book-entry registration of ownership would provide a modern, efficient answer to the market's needs.

However, the global note suffers from a number of inherent limitations.

First, the absence of physical notes may mean that the investor has less protection in the event of a default on payment under the programme. He may also find it harder to pledge his holding as collateral for a loan. Secondly, the global note system in its purest form requires all owners of the note to keep their 'paper' in an account with the global note agent, generally one of the major clearing systems, and physical delivery is impossible. To overcome these two problems, global note programmes may provide for investors to request the production of physical notes at any time. In some versions, definitive notes are printed in advance and issued on request. However, to the extent that this occurs, the cost benefits of a global note will be reduced and of course it requires a stock of security printed notes to be held by the issuing agent for each programme. A third problem is that it is not possible to clear the global note in the UK as any transfer of ownership would attract stamp duty under existing UK tax rules.

(iii) Universal notes

This is a new product developed by the First Chicago Clearing Centre. It aims to combine the benefits of both conventional definitives and global notes, while avoiding certain of the problems associated with both methods. Universal notes compare with conventional definitives in four important respects:

(i)   they are bearer notes (with the same legal status as conventional definitive notes) capable of being issued in denominations and maturities required by the most flexible programme. Each note is serially numbered and complete in all essential legal respects;

(ii) the notes are issued on continuous, perforated plain stationery mounted on a computer-printer (it is *not* security-paper);

(iii) the notes are in standardised formats suitable for a wide range of issuers;

(iv) the notes, as long as they are retained in the clearing system, are not security-printed. As long as physical delivery is not required, there is no risk of loss through theft or forgery since universal notes will be kept under the same standard of care as conventional definitive bearer notes.

The combination of these factors enables high-speed, low-cost volume issuing techniques to be exploited and may reduce the 'per note' cost of issuing by as much as 80%.

If physical delivery of the note is subsequently required, the 'Universal Note' is cancelled and replaced by a security-printed note. The cost of this is passed back to the issuer. However, since the security-printed version is also in a standard format, the issuer does not need to have notes specially printed for his programme and the issuing agent avoids the cost of holding in its vaults a separate stock of notes for each programme.

TYPES OF NOTE: SUMMARY
Conventional definitives

Advantages	*Disadvantages*
1 Tried and tested method.	1 Relatively expensive, especially for low denominations or short maturities.
2 Acceptable to all investors.	2 Issuing of security-printed notes is hard to automate.
3 Allows for physical delivery.	3 Individual stock of notes needed for each issuer.

Global notes

Advantages	*Disadvantages*
1 'Paperless' system cuts cost of issuing.	1 Resistance from some investors to absence of bearer notes.
2 Book-entry system means no paper flows to track.	2 Delivery outside clearing system may not be possible.
	3 Providing for definitive options means that costs of printing and storage are not totally avoided.

Universal notes

Advantages	*Disadvantages*
1 System allows for streamlined, automated issuing, hence cost is competitive with global notes.	1 Note format is standardised, which may be restrictive for issuers with special requirements.
2 Investors own bearer notes at all times.	2 Physical delivery – where needed – requires replacement note which reduces cost advantage.
3 System allows for delivery outside clearing system if needed.	

SELECTING THE CLEARING SYSTEM

We should now consider the criteria governing the selection of the clearing system. The investor makes the choice of clearing system. It will decide in which system it wishes to hold its paper – or whether it prefers to hold it outside the established clearing systems, at its bank or elsewhere. The investor may well be influenced in its choice by the circumstances of the purchase – if it has no strong preference for one clearing system or another, it may choose to leave the securities in the system where they originated. What frequently happens in practice, however, is that the dealers – often the initial purchasers of the paper – will take note of where their investors wish to hold the paper and will hold their own paper, pending a sale, in the same system or in another system providing efficient access to that system. The ability to transfer paper safely, efficiently and inexpensively to its ultimate destination is especially important to the dealer who will be largely bearing the costs of the transaction. Therefore, one criterion for the choice of clearing system that is relevant to the dealer is: where is the paper likely to end up?

However, there are a number of other criteria important to all parties in selecting a clearing system:

(i) Reliability

This is probably the most important single aspect. Reliability can best be measured by the proportion of transactions that fail to be completed on the due date. Sometimes this will be due to circumstances outside the system's control (e g an expected inward delivery of securities did not materialise). However, the clearing systems with the best record of avoiding fails are those which make every effort to:

(i)   match instructions from both parties before processing takes place; and
(ii) in the event of a discrepancy, contact the parties concerned by telephone to resolve the problem.

(ii) Market coverage

Clearly, the greater the proportion of market participants willing to hold their securities in a clearing system, the less need for physical delivery and the greater the benefits that that system is able to offer to each individual participant.

(iii) Cut-off times

As with issuing and paying agency, the later the deadlines established by a clearing system for receipt of instructions and incoming securities, the more flexibility and scope is offered to its participants. Cut-off times vary by system and can be as late as 5.00 pm London time for receipt of instructions, to effect settlement on the same day.

(iv) Special features such as assured payment

Some clearing systems offer an assurance of payment on behalf of all purchases made by their participants. In other words, the seller, whether itself a participant or an entity outside the system, is assured of receiving payment from the clearing system for sales of securities to a participant. The clearing system is able to assure payment without undue risk by having a lien over the securities held in its participant's accounts for payments made by it in this way. Some systems do not provide the assurance, but will only provide funds to the seller if sufficient funds, or other collateral, are held in the buyer's account in advance of payment taking place. Thus there is less certainty of settlement.

SAME-DAY SETTLEMENT

The period of time from the striking of a deal between the seller and the buyer (or between the issuer and the dealer) and payment of funds in exchange for the securities is known as the settlement period.

Settlement periods vary according to markets. For example, for domestic commercial paper, same-day settlement is the norm. That is, the deal is struck and settled on the same day. The same is true for sterling CDs and sterling commercial paper, provided the deal is struck by 12.30 pm. After 12.30 pm, settlement takes place the following day. On Euro-commercial paper settlement is generally on a two-day basis. For example, a deal struck on Monday is settled on Wednesday. The practice of settling two (business) days after the deal is struck is known as 'spot' settlement. Settlement practice in the Euro-commercial paper market is thus similar to that employed in foreign exchange dealings and the Euro-CD market. By contrast, Eurobonds are normally settled on a seven-day basis.

The problem with spot settlement in the Euro-commercial paper market is that it does not always suit the requirements of the various parties to the deal. In particular, issuers which have programmes in both the domestic commercial paper and the Euro-commercial paper markets frequently prefer same-day settlement. The borrower will wish to issue paper in one market or the other according to market conditions, which generally means whenever it can obtain the better rate for its paper on any given day. In order to compare rates on a satisfactory basis, settlement periods in both markets should be in alignment. However, this is not possible since the domestic commercial paper market is same-day and the Euro-commercial paper market is generally two-day settlement. Since a large body of issuers required it same-day settlement began to be introduced in the Euro-commercial paper market in early 1985.

A late cut-off time for receipt of instructions is essential if same-day settlement is to be of practical benefit to an issuer. The five-hour time difference between London and New York means that, if the issuer wants to examine rates in the domestic commercial paper market, it is mid- to late afternoon in London by the time the issuer can make its decision in which market to issue.

There is a certain amount of controversy over whether same-day settlement is of genuine benefit to the issuer. Advocates claim that it offers the issuer the prospect of lowering its overall cost of funds by, effectively, being able to arbitrage between the two major commercial paper markets. Sceptics argue that same-day settlement is not necessary for this purpose, and that dealers should be able to give a reliable indication of rates the previous day.

A further limitation to the benefits of same-day settlement lies in the fact that, irrespective of issuer preferences, most Euro-commercial paper *investors* still expect to settle on a two-day basis. Most competing Euro-instruments (CDs, time-deposits) settle on a two-day basis. This means that the dealer will be buying same-day and selling two-day. Even if the dealer on-sells the securities immediately (perhaps unlikely if the deal is struck late afternoon in London) the dealer will have to fund its position for two days. Some dealers are less willing to do this than others for both risk and profitability reasons. Same-day settlement applies today to only a very small proportion of the total transactions in the Euro-commercial paper market.

ISSUING AND PAYING AGENCY: THE RISKS

Because it is involved in the flows of funds at both issuing and maturity, the issuing and paying agent is exposed to a certain amount of risk. These flows of funds are frequently of large magnitude, up to $100 million or more on occasions. An issuing and paying agent therefore has to analyse and assess the exposures carefully and decide on the extent to which it is prepared to carry such risks as well as ensuring, naturally, that where risks are incurred, an adequate remuneration is earned.

(i) Risks at issuing

The issuing agent delivers securities to the initial purchaser against payment. This payment is remitted to the issuer.

An exposure arises because, in general, it will not be operationally practical for the agent to ascertain that funds have been received before funds are paid away. US dollar funds payments are made to the agent's New York office. The New York payments system, CHIPS, opens at 8.30 am and closes at 4.30 pm Eastern time (1.30 pm and 9.30 pm respectively London time). Therefore, payments may frequently be received after close of business in London. The incoming funds cannot, therefore, be monitored effectively by the agent in London. It is also, in general, not practical for the agent's New York office to monitor the payments because of the large volume of payment instructions handled: there will be no obvious way of linking the expected incoming payments with the outgoing ones. Therefore the general practice is for the agent to accept an intra-day exposure when securities are issued. If payment is not received, for any reason, from the note purchasers, the agent will be out of funds.

However, the agent's position is protected to a large extent by the following two practices:

(i) Where notes are physically delivered to the purchasers, the agent will release the securities against an unconditional undertaking, signed by the purchaser's bank, to make payment for the securities *as principal*. This means that the ultimate risk of non-payment is a risk on that bank, not on the purchaser. The agent will normally establish a 'delivery limit' for the amount of securities it will deliver to each individual bank on any one day. In practice, these limits will be high enough to cover normal volumes of business, certainly in the case of the major London banks.

(ii) Where notes are retained by the agent in safekeeping on behalf of the purchasers (as will be the case where the agent operates a clearing system), the contract signed by the participants in that system will normally stipulate that the agent has a lien over the securities in the participant's account for any payments not received in respect of purchases. In other words, if the purchaser defaults in paying the agent, the agent can in due course sell, or hold to maturity, the securities and realise the funds.

In relying on this, the agent is of course relying on the value of the underlying securities. The risk, therefore is on the *issuer*. The agent will usually stipulate which issuers' securities are regarded as acceptable collateral for this purpose. To summarise, in this situation the agent's recourse is first to the purchaser, second to the issuer.

(ii) Risks at maturity

The paying agent pays noteholders at maturity on presentation of their notes, and receives payment from the issuer.

An exposure arises in the same way as in the issuing process, except that the flows of funds are reversed. The agent's risk is that the issuer will fail to reimburse it, having itself paid funds to the noteholders. The agent's exposure, therefore, is an intra-day settlement risk on the issuer. No recourse is available to other parties. The agent has no basis for reclaiming funds from the noteholders.

The agent can reduce or avoid this exposure in a number of ways, for example:

(i) by requiring the issuer to pay the funds one day before maturity date. This of course completely removes any risk on the agent's part. Normally, the issuer will require the agent to pay interest on these funds, on which the agent has overnight use. Generally, issuers are reluctant to pay in advance unless some other source of funds is readily available to them; or

(ii) by limiting the amount of paper that can mature on any single day. This amount will be a figure that the agent is comfortable in accepting as an intra-day settlement risk on the issuer; or

(iii) by ensuring that the issuing and paying agreement provides that the agent can delay paying noteholders until it is satisfied that payment has been received from the issuer. This would be a drastic step to take but, clearly, an agent would be entitled to invoke this clause if it became concerned about the solvency of an issuer on maturity date.

EXISTING CLEARING SYSTEMS FOR EURO-COMMERCIAL PAPER

There are four major clearing systems currently involved in the clearing of Euro-commercial paper: one is Brussels-based (Euroclear), one is situated in

Luxembourg (Cedel) and two are London-based systems (First Chicago Clearing Centre and Chase Manhattan Bank NA).

Euroclear and Cedel are predominantly clearers of long-term securities such as Eurobonds and FRNs. They have in recent years been expanding their range of clearing operations, including Euro-commercial paper. Both systems utilise a network of depository banks in various countries. These depository banks safekeep the securities and receive and deliver them when physical movement is required. Euroclear and Cedel themselves are purely *clearing* operations: receiving instructions from participants, maintaining the accounts of participants, instructing the depositories to receive or deliver the securities, and receiving and paying funds. They do not physically handle the securities themselves.

One other feature of both systems is that their clearing operations have been primarily designed for the longer settlement periods of bonds. Both have adapted their operations to service the Euro-commercial paper market, particularly in the provision of same-day settlement capabilities.

A strength of both systems in servicing Euro-commercial paper has been the large number of investors willing to hold their securities in these systems. A possible disadvantage, however, relative to the London-based systems, has been their greater remoteness from London.

First Chicago and Chase are both specialists in short-term money market instruments. They were set up originally to service the Euro-CD market and found the transition to Euro-commercial paper a natural extension of those activities. While the CD clearing market is still competed for, it is in Euro-commercial paper that the competition between the systems has been most fierce.

While competition is healthy and a spur to innovation and responsive service, the fragmentation between the four clearing systems has been a source of concern amongst market participants. In response to market needs, the clearing systems have been establishing electronic links which enable the delivery of securities to be effected from one system to another without the costs, risks and uncertainty of physical movement.

The first such link was established between Euroclear and Cedel. Originally, this electronic 'bridge' was designed for the movement of bonds. However, it can also be used for Euro-commercial paper and other short-term instruments. The second link was established between Chase and Cedel at the beginning of 1986. Chase became a London depository for Cedel for short-term paper which enabled customers using the Chase system to sell their securities to Cedel customers without need for physical delivery. The securities remain physically in Chase's vaults but are transferred to the books of Cedel. Although not a clearing system, Citibank in London was also appointed a Cedel depository which also enables Citibank, acting as issuing and paying agent, to issue securities direct to the Cedel investor base.

The third link to be put in place became operational from 1 October 1986. The First Chicago Clearing Centre was appointed a London depository for the Euroclear system for short-term paper. In a similar way to the Chase/Cedel link, the FCCC/Euroclear link enables market participants to transfer Euro-commercial paper and other short-term instruments between the FCCC and Euroclear systems electronically.

Table 25

The Euro-commercial paper clearing process

TYPICAL SEQUENCE OF EVENTS

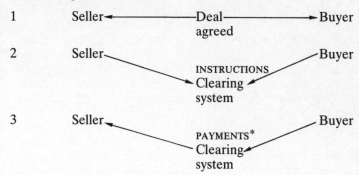

* net basis for each participant

Table 26

Issuing and paying agents

DIRECT ACCESS INTO CLEARING SYSTEMS (AS AT OCTOBER 1986)

	Clearing system links			
IPA	*Cedel*	*Chase*	*Euroclear*	*FCCC*
Chase Manhattan	X	X		
Citibank	X			
FCCC			X	X
Morgan Guaranty			X	

CHAPTER 7

Legal aspects

Buyers, sellers and issuers of euronotes and Euro-commercial paper are subject to a variety of laws and regulations relating primarily to withholding tax on interest and discount, instrument duties, income tax, disclosure/prospectus requirements and sales restrictions. The scope of this book is not such that would enable a complete review of the individual national laws and regulations governing the issue and purchase of notes in every country. This chapter therefore refrains from dealing with the domestic legal requirements of issuers and investors, but endeavours to focus on the legal framework surrounding the intermediaries between issuer and investor (though often concerning both the latter two) and the instrument itself.

The key legal considerations for professional dealers and for the generic instrument relate to (i) the possibility that notes come into contact with the United States and (ii) London as the principal financial centre for the sale and trading of notes. The effect of (i) is to open up the market to the implications of the United States Securities Act of 1933 and Federal Income Tax regulations and of (ii) to involve certain aspects of English law.

THE SITUATION IN THE US

(i) The Securities Act of 1933

(a) The registration requirements of the Securities Act

The United States Securities Act of 1933 (the 'Securities Act') establishes a comprehensive registration procedure for offerings of securities involving 'interstate commerce' or the use of the US mails. Briefly stated, this procedure contemplates that a so-called registration statement – consisting largely of a detailed prospectus – must be filed with the Securities and Exchange Commission (the 'SEC') before securities are offered or sold to the public, unless an exemption from the registration requirement is available.[1] It is lawful for an offer or sale of 'securities' to be made by an 'issuer' or by an 'underwriter' (being defined to include anyone purchasing the securities with a view to distribution thereof) without compliance with this registration procedure.

The Securities Act provides for two remedies for failure to comply with the registration requirement. Both the issuer and the underwriters may be subject to enforcement action by the SEC (which could include the imposition of

---

1 The person claiming an exemption from the registration requirement of the Securities Act bears the burden of establishing the availability of the exemption.

criminal penalties) and to action by a purchaser of the securities to rescind its purchase within one year from the date of sale. This right of rescission is based solely on improper failure to register, and has nothing to do with questions as to the accuracy or completeness of a prospectus or other offering materials.

The Securities Act was not written with a view to the special problems involved in offerings of securities in the international markets. The Securities Act was designed first and foremost to apply to offerings made by US corporations in the US; however, there is no explicit statutory recognition that the Securities Act does not apply with equal force (given, as a jurisdictional matter, a minimum degree of activity touching on the US) to an offering by a US corporation, as well as a non-US corporation or government, outside the US. The jurisdictional minimum degree of activity is defined in the Securities Act in terms of the use of the US mails or the use of instruments of transportation or communication in 'interstate commerce', i e the use of means of communication or transportation involving the US. What this means in practice is that a public offering that takes place entirely outside the US is beyond the reach of the registration requirements of the Securities Act; however, a single contact with the US, such as an offer made from outside the US by telephone or letter to a person in the US, may, at least in theory, make the entire transaction subject to all of the requirements of the Securities Act.

(b) Exemptions from registration under the Securities Act

At present, as a matter of market practice, euronotes and Euro-commercial paper are not registered under the Securities Act. Accordingly, euronotes and Euro-commercial paper (collectively, 'short-term obligations') of both US and non-US issuers are usually offered and sold only under circumstances designed to ensure that such offers and sales qualify for an exemption from registration.

There are several exemptions from the registration requirements of the Securities Act that may be available to an issue of short-term obligations. Four of the principal exemptions are discussed below.

A. THE IMPLIED FOREIGN OFFERING EXEMPTION

The exemption most commonly relied on in the Euromarkets is the 'implied foreign offering exemption' which was announced by the SEC on 9 July 1964 in Release No 33–4708 (the '4708 Release'). In the 4708 Release, the SEC acknowledged that the Securities Act was not intended to regulate the offer and sale by a US issuer of debt securities outside the US to non-US persons and accordingly concluded that an offering of debt securities would be exempt from registration under the Securities Act if made 'under circumstances reasonably designed to preclude distribution or redistribution of the securities within, or to nationals of, the United States' and if the distribution was effected 'in a manner which will result in the securities coming to rest abroad'. The SEC staff has taken a similar position with respect to an offering outside the US by a non-US issuer.[2]

2 This discussion addresses the problems relating to the issuance of debt securities and not equity. Equity securities of both US and non-US issuers issued in the Euromarkets are issued under procedures which differ substantially from the procedures discussed here for the issuance of debt.

Since the standard to be met ('circumstances reasonably designed') is, in part, a subjective one, the measures which must be taken in structuring an offering of securities outside the US in order to have the desired result (ie the securities 'coming to rest abroad') vary markedly depending on the facts. Relevant factors include whether the issuer is a US or non-US entity and whether there is an existing market in the US for its securities. Measures which may be 'reasonably designed' in the case of a non-US issuer unknown in the US may prove insufficient for a publicly traded US company or a non-US issuer which has an active market in the US for its securities.

Accordingly, while US issuers seeking to take advantage of the 'implied foreign offering exemption' have taken rather elaborate contractual and procedural measures for Eurobond issues (such as deferring, for a specified 'lock-up' period, delivery to the purchasers of the definitive securities and conditioning such eventual delivery on certification from the purchasers of their status as non-US persons), it has generally been thought adequate for many non-US issuers to take less rigorous measures.

Typically, in the case of Eurobond issues, these measures include statements in the offering documents to the effect that the securities have not been registered under the Securities Act and the imposition of contractual restrictions requiring underwriters and securities dealers participating in the distribution not to offer or sell the securities in the US or to US persons as part of the distribution of the securities. Also, in some instances, the measures have included an agreement not to sell securities acquired in the secondary market in the US or to US nationals or residents for a fixed period (most commonly 90 days) after the date on which the distribution is completed (as determined by the lead underwriter).

Euronotes and Euro-commercial paper raise a particular problem under the Securities Act that is not present in the case of Eurobonds. Since it it expected that issuers may wish to issue euronotes and Euro-commercial paper from time to time, the SEC could take the position that an issuer is engaged in a continuous distribution of the obligations. The normal measures taken in a Eurobond issue by US issuers and non-US issuers are not applicable to a continuous distribution since such measures are based on the premise that the distribution of a single, discrete issue of securities is being made and therefore that such securities can come to rest abroad. Accordingly, in the context of a continuous offering, the contractual restrictions on sales into the US or to US persons could never be terminated as they can in the case of a normal Eurobond issue.

Until recently, the SEC had not provided any guidance as to the measures that should be taken with respect to short-term obligations in order for such obligations to qualify for the 'implied foreign offering exemption'. However, on 13 February 1985, the SEC issued the *First Interstate Bancorp* no-action letter in which it confirmed that certain procedures outlined in the request for the no-action letter were appropriate in applying the 4708 Release to short-term obligations.[3] The *First Interstate* letter is the only expression of the SEC staff's views on arrangements designed for short-term obligations to meet the

---

3 Under the euronote issuance facility described in the *First Interstate* letter, the underwriting banks were obligated to purchase euronotes which the issuer decided to issue. There was no tender panel or placing agent to which the notes were first offered.

implied foreign offering exemption embodied in the 4708 Release. Accordingly, a Euro-commercial paper programme or euronote issuance facility that is intended to comply with this exemption should be structured generally along the lines set forth in that letter. Briefly stated, those procedures contemplate that:

(i) the maturities of the obligations will be short-term (ie not more than one year);[4]

(ii) the securities will be in minimum denominations of US $500,000 (or the equivalent in another currency);[5]

(iii) the dealer will agree not to offer or sell the securities (whether acquired as part of the initial distribution or otherwise) directly or indirectly in the US or to US persons (except, subject to certain limitations, to foreign branches of US banks and to US persons acting as agents, custodians or fiduciaries acting pursuant to specific instructions and without investment discretion on behalf of non-US persons);[6]

(iv) the dealer will deliver a written confirmation (generally as part of, or together with, the confirmation of sale) to each purchaser of securities whereby the purchaser agrees to certain restrictions on the offer and sale of the securities and to deliver such confirmation to any subsequent purchasers (such requirement often being referred to as 'cascading confirmations', ie cascading from purchaser to purchaser); and

(v) the securities will bear a Securities Act legend indicating that the obligations have not been registered under the Securities Act and, except in certain limited circumstances, may not be offered or sold in the US or to US persons.

A no-action letter is a letter issued by the staff of the SEC (but not by the SEC itself) stating that the staff will not recommend to the SEC that the SEC take action for failure to register the offering. In theory, such a letter has no legal effect; it does not preclude the staff from subsequently making such a recommendation, nor does it preclude the SEC, acting with or without such a recommendation, from taking action. It also does not preclude, as a legal matter, a third party, such as a purchaser of securities, from claiming that the offering should have been registered and from seeking to rescind his purchase on that ground. A no-action letter is nonetheless of value since it provides, as a practical matter, assurance that if the arrangements for an offering are described in the request for the no-action letter the SEC will not take action against the issuer and the underwriters, even though others involved in the distribution may, in fact, sell securities in the US or to US investors as part of the distribution.

4 Although the notes in the *First Interstate* letter were of three- and six-month maturities, the procedures outlined in that letter have been applied to programmes providing for the issuance of obligations with maturities of up to a year. However, in the case of US issuers, the maturity of the obligations generally must be limited to 183 days if interest or discount on the obligations is to be exempt from US withholding tax.

5 This can probably be reduced to US $100,000. However, as described more fully below, short-term obligations of US issuers and certain non-US issuers must be issued in denominations of at least $500,000 in order to be exempt from US information reporting and backup withholding tax requirements.

6 Although the *First Interstate* letter specifies that the agent must act without discretion, in the *Baer Securities Corporation* no-action letter by the SEC on 12 September 1979 the SEC took a no-action position with respect to a US agent proposing to acquire Eurobonds for non-US clients for whom such agent had discretion.

Also, in the *First Interstate* letter the SEC stated that such agents and custodians must be US corporations registered with the SEC as broker-dealers. However, a number of programmes are presently being marketed which instead require only that such agents or custodians be located outside the US.

B. THE COMMERCIAL PAPER EXEMPTION

Under s 3(a)(3) of the Securities Act, short-term obligations that satisfy certain requirements may qualify as 'commercial paper' that is exempt from registration. To qualify for the commercial paper exemption, short-term obligations must have the following characteristics:

(i) The obligations must have a maturity that does not exceed nine months.
(ii) The obligations must be of prime quality. Issuers have customarily satisfied this requirement on the basis of ratings of their commercial paper by the nationally recognised rating services in the US.[7]
(iii) The obligations must be of a type not ordinarily purchased by the general public. This requirement can normally be satisfied if the commercial paper is issued in denominations of at least US $100,000 and placed without public advertising with institutions that would qualify as purchasers in a private placement.
(iv) The obligations must be issued to facilitate 'current transactions'. In cases where the proceeds will be used to finance inventory or accounts receivable or for other working capital purposes, compliance with this condition is clear. In some cases, the SEC staff has issued no-action letters where the proceeds of the issuance of commercial paper have not been traced to particular uses, on the basis of an agreement by the issuer to limit the commercial paper outstanding at any time to an amount based on a formula.[8] Interim financing of acquisitions is not deemed to be a 'current transaction'.

Short-term obligations meeting these four conditions would qualify as 'commercial paper' exempt from Securities Act registration. Consequently, for purposes of the Securities Act, such short-term obligations could be freely sold in the US (subject, of course, to the restrictions imposed by clause (iii) above). Despite the apparent advantages, at present few issuers have issued short-term obligations qualifying for the commercial paper exemption. There are two principal reasons. First, an issuer may not want to restrict the use of proceeds to current transactions. Second, as described more fully below, exempt commercial paper of US issuers must comply with certain additional certification requirements (the so-called TEFRA 'B' requirements) in order to establish an exemption from US information reporting requirements and backup withholding tax. These requirements are more exacting than those required to comply with the implied foreign offering exemption, and some dealers have expressed the view that these certification requirements reduce the marketability of the obligations.[9]

7 It may be possible in certain circumstances to meet this requirement without ratings if the issuer and the dealer are of the view that the commercial paper would, if rated, be rated in the highest category.
8 The 'current transactions' requirement is a complicated subject beyond the scope of this discussion.
9 In addition, certain issuers may in any case insist on US selling restrictions to maintain separate markets for their Euro-commercial paper and their commercial paper sold in the US in which case the advantage of being freely issuable in the US vanishes.
    The tax issues relevant to the marketing of Euro-commercial paper are not a concern in the commercial paper market in the United States where compliance with US information reporting requirements is taken for granted.

C. THE BANK EXEMPTION

Under the Securities Act, s 3(a)(2) 'any security issued or guaranteed by any bank' is exempt from registration. The Securities Act defines a 'bank' as 'any national bank, or any banking institution organised under the laws of any State, territory, or the District of Columbia, the business of which is substantially confined to banking and is supervised by the State or territorial banking commission or similar official'. Accordingly, short-term obligations (including certificates of deposit) offered and sold by a US bank are exempt from Securities Act registration. Further, in the case of branches of foreign banks located in New York State and certain other states, the SEC staff has taken a no-action position with respect to the availability of the exemption for an offering of securities by such branches. This position is based upon the conclusion that the US branch is subject to substantially the same regulation by the relevant banking authorities as domestic banks located in the state in question.[10] As a result, short-term obligations offered and sold by a US branch of a foreign bank should generally be considered as securities exempt from registration under the Securities Act.[11]

For purposes of the Securities Act, such obligations, being exempt securities, may be offered and sold without any US selling restrictions. However, as is the case with commercial paper, special US selling restrictions would be necessary in order for such obligations to be exempt from US information reporting requirements and backup withholding tax.

D. THE PRIVATE PLACEMENT EXEMPTION

The Securities Act, s 4(2) contains an exemption for 'transactions by an issuer not involving any public offering', commonly known as the 'private placement' exemption. A private placement under the Securities Act is not merely a sale to a limited number of purchasers without the use of an underwriting syndicate. Through SEC rules, interpretative releases, no-action letters and court decisions, a complex body of law and regulation has developed as to what constitutes a private placement.[12]

Although it is difficult as a general matter to specify the precise circumstances in which the private placement exemption is available, certain characteristics must be present. Briefly, a private placement is an offering of securities which is made only to a limited number of offerees who (i) are

10 If the US branch is located in a state as to which the SEC staff has not taken this position, it may be desirable to obtain a no-action letter from the SEC staff before proceeding with an offering of obligations of such branch.

There is reason to believe that the SEC staff may be reconsidering its position with respect to the applicability of s 3(a)(2) to securities of US branches of foreign banks, but the SEC staff has yet to announce any change in its position.

11 Short-term obligations of a corporation backed by a letter of credit of a US bank or a US branch would also be exempt.

Section 3(a)(2) of the Securities Act also exempts from the registration requirements any security issued or guaranteed by the US or any state or political subdivision therein.

12 It should be noted that the kind of transaction commonly referred to as a private placement in Europe – that is the sale of securities to a small number of banks which intend to place them with their own clients – seldom constitutes a private placement for the purposes of the Securities Act, s 4(2).

purchasing for their own account and not for resale and (ii) have access to sufficient information concerning the issuer and have sufficient skill in financial matters to be able to evaluate the risk of the investment being made. Each purchaser in a private placement would usually be required to deliver an investment letter setting forth certain restrictions on its resale of the obligations and to give certain representations as to its status as a sophisticated investor. This contrasts with the cascading confirmation procedure generally used for euronotes and Euro-commercial paper issued pursuant to the implied foreign offering exemption.

The SEC and the courts interpret the private placement exemption strictly; it is established law that a transaction which, taken in isolation, satisfies the requirements of the exemption may be subject to the registration requirement if it is part of a larger offering or a series of related transactions which should be 'integrated' to determine if the exemption is available. The factors considered relevant to this determination are whether (i) the different offerings are part of a single plan of financing, (ii) the offerings involve the issuance of the same class of security, (iii) the offerings are made at or about the same time and (iv) the offerings are made for the same general purpose.

Because of the principle of integration, every sale in the US or to US persons must meet the test of s 4(2); if any sale in the US or to a US person fails to qualify for the private placement exemption, the entire transaction would fall outside the exemption. In the 4708 Release, which recognised the implied foreign offering exemption, the SEC took the position that transactions otherwise meeting the requirements of the private placement exemption are not subject to the registration requirement solely because an offering outside the US which satisfies the requirements for the implied foreign offering exemption is being made concurrently with a private placement in the US. Accordingly, a private placement can be coupled with the implied foreign offering exemption so that offers and sales of short-term obligations may be made within the US or to US persons on the basis of the s 4(2) exemption and outside the US to non-US persons on the basis of the implied foreign offering exemption.

A programme combining private placements and sales based on the implied foreign offering exemption should have certain additional elements: (i) the securities sold to the US investors should be issued only in registered (rather than bearer) form, with a special Securities Act legend; (ii) the securities should be in minimum denominations of US $500,000 (or the equivalent in any other currency);[13] (iii) each US investor should be required to deliver an investment letter to the dealer;[14] and (iv) the investors outside the US purchasing bearer obligations pursuant to the implied foreign offering exemption should be required to present certificates of non-US beneficial

---

13 US $500,000 is the denomination most commonly recommended by US counsel. However, it may be acceptable in certain circumstances to have a lower minimum denomination.
14 An alternative, but less desirable, procedure would be for the dealer to deliver a confirmation to each US investor whereby the investor is deemed to make such representations and agreements. In either case, the securities could be transferred only if the registrar for the securities received a letter to such effect from the transferee.

ownership at maturity in order to receive payment.[15] These additional restrictions are those most commonly found in Euro-commercial paper programmes and euronote issuance facilities which permit private placements.[16]

(ii) US federal income tax considerations

A prospective issuer of euronotes or Euro-commercial paper must address three separate US federal income tax considerations.[17] First, the issuer must ensure that interest and discount on the obligations may be paid to non-US investors free of the 30% withholding tax imposed by the US on certain payments of US source interest or discount to non-US persons. Second, in the case of obligations issued in bearer form, the issuer must ensure that the obligations are exempt from the registration requirements of the Tax Equity and Fiscal Responsibility Act of 1982 ('TEFRA'). Third, the issuer must consider whether to structure the euronote facility or Euro-commercial paper programme so that payments on the euronotes or Euro-commercial paper are exempt from US information reporting and backup withholding tax requirements. Each of these three considerations is discussed more fully below.

(a) US withholding tax

A. IN GENERAL

In general, the US imposes a 30% withholding tax on payments to non-US persons of interest or discount arising from sources within the US.[18] Interest or discount ordinarily will be treated as arising from sources within the US if the interest or discount is paid on (i) an obligation issued by a US corporation, or (ii) an obligation issued by a non-US corporation if the issuer (A) derives at least 50% of its aggregate gross income for a specified period from the conduct of a US trade or business or (B) is a US branch of a non-US bank. Accordingly, interest or discount paid on euronotes or Euro-commercial paper of a US issuer or a non-US issuer of a type described in the preceding sentence will be subject to US withholding tax unless an exemption is available under the Internal Revenue Code or a US income tax treaty.[19]

15 Sales to foreign branches of US banks also are made on the basis of the s 4(2) exemption, but on the basis of various no-action letters, including *First Interstate*, the additional restrictions required in the text are not required for such sales.
16 Depending on the circumstances, these restrictions may be loosened to accommodate marketing requirements. For instance, a more relaxed approach may be acceptable for a non-US issuer that does not have any securities actively traded in the US.
17 In addition, a prospective issuer that has connections with a non-US jurisdiction (such as a non-US corporation or a foreign branch of a US corporation) must consider the tax laws of that other jurisdiction. Ordinarily, the primary concern would be to ensure that payments are exempt from withholding tax.
18 This 30% withholding tax does not apply to payments of interest or discount that are effectively connected with a US trade or business conducted by the non-US person; such payments instead are taxed by the US on a net income basis as part of the income of the US trade or business.
19 Under legislation recently passed by the United States Congress, any interest or discount that is deducted by a foreign corporation in computing the taxable income of its US trade or business will be treated as arising from sources within the United States. Accordingly, broadly speaking, interest or discount paid on euronotes or Euro-commercial paper of a US branch of any non-US corporation will be subject to US withholding tax unless a statutory or treaty exemption is available.

The exemption from US withholding tax that is of primary importance for euronotes and Euro-commercial paper is the exemption provided by the Internal Revenue Code for original issue discount on notes having a maturity at issue of 183 days or less.[20] Notes having a maturity of more than 183 days but not more than one year generally are subject to the 30% US withholding tax unless the beneficial owner of the notes is entitled to the benefits of a US income tax treaty that eliminates US withholding tax on interest. Not all non-US investors are entitled to the benefits of such a treaty and, in any case, the procedures required to claim treaty benefits are inconsistent with the anonymity ordinarily required by non-US investors. Accordingly, the maturity of euronotes or Euro-commercial paper issued by a US corporation (or by a non-US corporation the interest and discount payments of which are considered to arise from sources within the US) ordinarily is limited to 183 days.[21]

It is customary for euronotes and Euro-commercial paper of such an issuer to provide that the issuer will indemnify non-US investors for US withholding taxes that may be imposed (other that US withholding taxes imposed by reason of a failure to comply with applicable certification, information or other reporting requirements concerning the holder or beneficial owner of the euronotes or Euro-commercial paper (so-called 'backup' withholding taxes)), *provided* that the investors do not have any of certain specified contacts with the US.

B. SPECIAL CONSIDERATIONS ARISING FROM THE COMMITTED NATURE OF A EURONOTE ISSUANCE FACILITY

In general, euronotes and Euro-commercial paper of a US issuer do not raise US withholding tax concerns because the credit extended to the issuer by each purchaser of a note is limited to 183 days. Accordingly, the interest or discount paid on the notes qualifies for the exemption from US withholding tax for discount obligations having a maturity of 183 days or less and the more complex rules that govern the exemption from US withholding tax for so-called 'portfolio interest' on obligations having a maturity of more than one year are not implicated.

In contrast to the ordinary purchaser of a note, however, the managing banks in an underwritten euronote issuance facility extend credit to the issuer for the life of the facility; any purchase by a manager of a particular short-term euronote is made pursuant to this long-term extension of credit. Accordingly, it is possible to make a forceful argument that euronotes purchased by the managers in a euronote issuance facility should not qualify for the exemption from US withholding tax for discount obligations with a maturity of 183 days or

---

20 Under a regulatory interpretation, interest paid at maturity on notes issued in interest-bearing form is treated as discount that may qualify for this exemption.

21 A second exemption from US withholding tax that is of lesser importance for euronotes and Euro-commercial paper is the exemption provided by the Internal Revenue Code for interest on deposit obligations issued by persons carrying on a banking business in the US. Under this exemption, a US bank or a US branch of a non-US bank may issue short-term deposit obligations free of US withholding tax, without any requirement that the maturity of the obligations be limited to 183 days.

less because, in the hands of the managers, those euronotes represent periodic drawings on a long-term credit facility rather than mere short-term notes.

In 1984, the United States Internal Revenue Service indicated that it would adopt this argument. In particular, the Internal Revenue Service released a General Counsel's Memorandum (the 'GCM')[22] indicating that euronotes that could not be placed by a tender agent and were sold to the managers in a long-term euronote issuance facility pursuant to the commitment of the managers to purchase notes should be treated for US federal income tax purposes as short-term participations in a long-term obligation rather than as mere short-term notes. Accordingly, the GCM suggested that euronotes purchased by the managers would not qualify for the exemption from US withholding tax for discount obligations having a maturity of 183 days or less.

The GCM has no application to euronotes sold to the tender panel members in a euronote issuance facility (or to Euro-commercial paper, where the dealer has no obligation to purchase any notes). In a typical euronote issuance facility, tender panel members are not contractually committed to purchase notes or to renew or roll over notes that they have purchased. Accordingly, euronotes purchased by tender panel members should not be subject to recharacterisation under the GCM as participations in a long-term credit facility and should continue to qualify for exemption from US withholding tax as discount obligations having a maturity of 183 days or less.[23]

However, the GCM suggests that euronotes sold to the managers will not qualify for the exemption from US withholding tax for discount notes having a maturity of 183 days or less. The position of the GCM is not limited to euronotes sold to the managers that in fact are rolled over by the sale of new euronotes to the managers, but extends to all euronotes sold to the managers where the contractual possibility of a rollover exists. Further, although the issue is not entirely clear, it is possible that the position of the GCM continues to apply to euronotes sold to the managers even after those euronotes are sold by the managers in the secondary market (that is, a euronote sold to a manager retains its character as a participation in a long-term extension of credit even in the hands of a secondary market purchaser).

Accordingly, the practical consequence of the issuance of the GCM is that a euronote issuance facility should be structured in a manner that allows euronotes sold to the managers to qualify for an exemption from US withholding tax even if those euronotes are treated as short-term participations in a long-term extension of credit. To ensure the availability of such an exemption, two separate measures should be taken. First, the euronote issuance facility should be structured in a manner that allows interest or discount paid on the euronotes to qualify for the exemption from US

22 A General Counsel's Memorandum is an internal memorandum written by the office of the Chief Counsel of the Internal Revenue Service with respect to issues arising in connection with a pending ruling. GCMs are not binding on taxpayers and do not have the force and effect of a published ruling.
23 However, in a case where a tender panel member is also, or is affiliated with, a manager, it is important that euronotes purchased by the tender panel member do *not* reduce the commitment of the manager on a dollar-for-dollar basis; any such dollar-for-dollar reduction could cause the short-term euronotes purchased by the tender panel member to be associated with the long-term extension of credit of the manager.

withholding tax for portfolio interest. Second, because euronotes purchased and held to maturity by the managers (that is, euronotes that are not resold by the managers in the secondary market) may not qualify for the portfolio interest exemption, each manager should establish its entitlement to an exemption from US withholding tax (ordinarily, under the terms of an applicable tax treaty).

1 Portfolio interest.   Assuming that euronotes sold to the managers are treated as participations in a long-term extension of credit, payments of interest and discount on those euronotes generally will qualify as portfolio interest exempt from US withholding tax if (i) the euronotes are issued in bearer form and (ii) the euronotes qualify for the 'Eurobond exception' to the anti-bearer bond rules enacted by TEFRA.

In general, TEFRA requires most debt securities in the US to be issued in registered form. To enforce this registration requirement, TEFRA imposes financial sanctions on issuers (whether US or non-US) and holders of 'registration-required' obligations that are in bearer form.

When TEFRA was under consideration, the United States Congress was made aware that the TEFRA registration requirement was incompatible with the preference of the Euromarket for bearer securities and anonymity. Accordingly, in order to prevent TEFRA from jeopardising access by US borrowers to the Euromarket, a Eurobond 'exception' was included in TEFRA; that is, notwithstanding the general registered form requirement of TEFRA, obligations that meet the requirements of this Eurobond exception may be issued in bearer form. The exemption from US withholding tax for portfolio interest builds on the Eurobond exception to TEFRA in the sense that bearer obligations must be issued in accordance with the Eurobond exception in order for interest or discount on the obligations to qualify as portfolio interest.

Under the Eurobond exception, an obligation may be issued in bearer form if (i) the obligation is issued under 'arrangements reasonably designed' to ensure that it is sold or resold in connection with the original issuance only to non-US persons, and (ii) so long as the obligation is in bearer form, (A) interest is payable on the obligation only outside the US and (B) a TEFRA legend appears on the obligation stating that any US person that holds the obligation in bearer form will be subject to limitations under US income tax laws (in particular, denial of capital gain treatment for any gain, and denial of a deduction for any loss, realised on the disposition of the obligation).

The requirements that must be met in order to establish that an obligation has been sold under 'arrangements reasonably designed' to ensure initial sales and resales only to non-US persons differ according to the manner in which the obligation is treated under the Securities Act. An obligation that is exempt from Securities Act registration under the implied foreign offering exemption will satisfy the 'arrangements reasonably designed' standard if (i) in connection with its original issuance, the obligation is offered for sale or resale, and delivered, only outside the US and (ii) the issuer, in reliance upon a written opinion of counsel received prior to the issuance of the obligation, determines that the obligation need not be registered under the Securities Act under the implied foreign offering exemption. The requirements described in the preceding sentence are commonly referred to as the 'TEFRA "A" requirements'.

By contrast, an obligation that is registered under the Securities Act, that is exempt from such registration under the Securities Act, s 3 or 4 or that is exempt from such registration by reason of not being a 'security' will satisfy the 'arrangements reasonably designed' standard only if the obligation meets a five-part test in connection with its original issuance: (i) the obligation must be offered for sale or resale, and delivered, only outside the US; (ii) the issuer must not, and each dealer must agree that it will not, offer to sell or resell the obligation in bearer form to any US person other than a financial institution that agrees to comply with certain reporting requirements; (iii) each purchaser of the obligation must receive a confirmation stating that the purchaser represents that it is not a US person (or is a financial institution that will comply with the relevant reporting requirements) and that, if it is a dealer, it will send similar confirmations to its purchasers; (iv) the obligation must be released in definitive form only upon presentation by the person entitled to physical delivery thereof of a certificate stating that the obligation is not being acquired by or on behalf of a US person (and that the obligation is not being acquired for offer to resell or for resale to a US person) or, if a beneficial interest is being acquired by a US person, that such US person is, or is acquiring the obligation through, a financial institution that will comply with the relevant reporting requirements; (v) the issuer or dealer that receives the certificate described in clause (iv) must not have actual knowledge that such certificate is false. The requirements described in the preceding sentence are commonly referred to as the 'TEFRA "B" requirements'. In the case of short-term obligations, the TEFRA 'B' requirements (including, in particular, the requirement that an obligation be delivered in definitive form only upon presentation of a certificate of non-US beneficial ownership by the person entitled to that delivery) are more exacting than the Securities Act requirements of the implied foreign offering exemption that are incorporated into the TEFRA 'A' requirements.

Assuming that euronotes sold to the managers are treated as participations in a long-term extension of credit, interest and discount on those euronotes generally will qualify as portfolio interest exempt from US withholding tax if the euronotes are issued in compliance with the requirements of the TEFRA Eurobond exception as described above. Accordingly, a secondary market participant that buys such euronotes from a manager may rely upon the portfolio interest exemption from US withholding tax if the exemption for discount notes having a maturity of 183 days or less is deemed to be unavailable.[24] However, for the reasons discussed below, euronotes actually held to maturity by the managers (that is, euronotes not sold by the managers in the secondary market) may not qualify for the portfolio interest exemption; accordingly, as described below, each manager in a euronote issuance facility must establish an individual exemption from US withholding tax.

24 However the portfolio interest exemption does not apply to obligations having a maturity of one year or less and, accordingly, obligations having a maturity greater than 183 days but not greater than one year cannot qualify either for the 183-day exemption or for the portfolio interest exemption. For this reason, issuers may wish to avoid selling euronotes to the managers during the period beginning one year prior to the termination of a euronote issuance facility and ending 184 days prior to that termination date.

2 The managers. In general, the exemption from US withholding tax for portfolio interest does not apply to interest or discount paid to a bank on an extension of credit made pursuant to a loan agreement entered into by the bank in the ordinary course of its trade or business. In most cases, euronote issuance facilities are treated by issuers as an alternative to revolving bank credit lines and, indeed, the managers in a euronote issuance facility usually are banks. Accordingly, there is a risk that if euronotes purchased and held to maturity by the managers are treated as participations in a long-term extension of credit, then interest or discount on those euronotes would be treated as interest paid to a bank pursuant to an extension of credit made in the ordinary course of the trade or business of the bank and accordingly, such interest or discount would not qualify as portfolio interest.

In order to deal with this risk, a euronote issuance facility should require each manager to establish in one of the following ways that it qualifies for an individual exemption from US withholding tax in respect of interest and discount paid on the euronotes. A manager may establish that it qualifies for the benefits of a US income tax treaty that eliminates US withholding tax on interest and discount. Alternatively, a manager may establish that interest and discount income received by it in respect of the euronotes will be effectively connected with a US trade or business conducted by it; such interest or discount will be exempt from US withholding tax but will be taxed by the US on a net income basis as part of the income of the US trade or business.

(a) TEFRA

As described above, TEFRA requires most debt securities in the US to be issued in registered form and imposes financial sanctions on issuers and holders of 'registration-required' obligations that are issued or held in bearer form. However, in general, TEFRA has very little direct importance for euronote issuance facilities and Euro-commercial paper programmes because obligations having a maturity at issue of one year or less are not 'registration-required' obligations and may be issued in bearer form. Nonetheless, TEFRA is of considerable indirect importance for a euronote issuance facility or Euro-commercial paper programme because (i) as described above, euronotes must be issued in compliance with the TEFRA 'A' requirements or the TEFRA 'B' requirements in order to establish that the euronotes qualify for the portfolio interest exemption from US withholding tax and (ii) as described below, euronotes and Euro-commercial paper must be issued in compliance with the TEFRA 'A' requirements or the TEFRA 'B' requirements in order to establish an exemption for the euronotes or Euro-commercial paper from US information reporting and backup withholding tax requirements.

(b) US information reporting and backup withholding tax requirements

A. IN GENERAL

In general, the US requires a payor of interest or principal on a debt obligation to file an information return with the Internal Revenue Service reporting the payment, and to withhold a 20% backup withholding tax from the payment if the payee fails to provide its taxpayer identification number. Broadly speaking, these information reporting and back-up withholding tax requirements apply both to the issuer of an obligation (and its paying agents) and to persons (such as custodians) that collect interest and principal payments and remit those payments to the beneficial owner. Thus, for example, if a paying agent makes a payment of interest to a custodian and the custodian remits that payment to the beneficial owner, then (i) the paying agent must file an information return reporting its payment to the custodian (and must withhold 20% of that payment if the custodian fails to provide its taxpayer identification number) and (ii) the custodian must file an information return reporting its payment to the beneficial owner (and must withhold 20% of *that* payment if the beneficial owner fails to provide *its* taxpayer identification number).

Non-US payees are exempt from information reporting and backup withholding tax (that is, a payor that makes a payment of interest or principal to a non-US payee need not file an information return with respect to that payment and backup withholding tax does not apply).[25] Ordinarily, however, a non-US payee must establish its exempt non-US status by providing to the payor an Internal Revenue Service Form W-8 (or, in the case of discount obligations with a maturity of 183 days or less, an Internal Revenue Service Form 1001) that contains the payee's name and address.

B. US ISSUERS AND NON-US ISSUERS WITH SUBSTANTIAL US CONNECTIONS: EXEMPT OBLIGATIONS

In recognition of the anonymity required by non-US investors, the Internal Revenue Service has issued regulations that permit US issuers and non-US issuers with a substantial US connection[26] to issue obligations that are largely exempt from information reporting and backup withholding tax without any need for non-US investors to furnish a Form W-8 or similar form. Under the regulations, as described more fully below, these 'exempt' obligations must be issued pursuant to procedural requirements that are designed to ensure that the obligations are sold outside of the US to non-US persons.[27]

1 Short-term discount obligations of US issuers and certain non-US issuers; short-term deposit obligations of US banks and US branches of non-US banks. The first class of short-term obligations that may qualify as exempt

---

25 Corporate payees also are exempt from information reporting and backup withholding tax. A payor may treat a payee as a corporation for this purpose if the name of the payee contains any of certain specified expressions of corporate status (or under certain other circumstances). However, a payor instead may choose to require corporate payees to provide a certificate establishing their exempt status. The relevant US regulations are not clear as to whether certain other payees (including, in particular, foreign governments, foreign central banks of issue, dealers in securities and financial institutions) also are exempt from information reporting and backup withholding tax.

26 For purposes of the discussion in the text, a non-US issuer has a 'substantial US connection' if the issuer (i) derives at least 50% of its aggregate gross income for a specified period from the conduct of a US trade or business; (ii) is a US branch of a non-US bank; or (iii) is a 'controlled foreign corporation'. Broadly speaking, a controlled foreign corporation is a foreign corporation more than 50% of the voting stock of which is held by 10% US shareholders. In effect, under the legislation described in footnote 19, a US branch of any non-US corporation would have a 'substantial US connection'.

27 The application of these procedural requirements to global notes raises certain special and highly technical issues, a discussion of which is beyond the scope of this chapter.

obligations includes (i) discount obligations of a US issuer (or of a non-US issuer that derives at least 50% of its aggregate gross income for a specified period from the conduct of a US trade or business) with a maturity of 183 days or less, and (ii) deposit obligations of a US bank or of a US branch of a non-US bank with a maturity of one year or less. Any such obligation will qualify as an exempt obligation only if: (i) interest and principal on the obligation are payable, and in fact are paid, only outside the US; (ii) the face amount of the obligation is not less than $500,000; (iii) the obligation is sold under 'arrangements reasonably designed' to ensure that it is sold or resold in connection with the original issuance only to non-US persons (that is, in practice, the obligation is issued under arrangements that satisfy the TEFRA 'A' requirements or the TEFRA 'B' requirements, as the case may be); (iv) any obligation in registered form is registered in the name of a corporation, dealer in securities, financial institution or similar institutional investor; and (v) a special legend appears on the obligation.[28]

2 Short-term obligations of controlled foreign corporations. The second class of short-term obligations that may qualify as exempt obligations includes obligations of a controlled foreign corporation with a maturity of one year or less. Any such obligation will qualify as an exempt obligation if and only if (i) interest and principal on the obligation are paid outside the US; (ii) the obligation is issued under arrangements that satisfy the TEFRA 'A' requirements or the TEFRA 'B' requirements, as the case may be; and (iii) any obligation in registered form is registered in the name of a corporation, dealer in securities, financial institution or similar institutional investor.

3 The information reporting and backup withholding tax regime applicable to an exempt obligation. If an obligation qualifies as an exempt obligation under the requirements set forth above, then payments on the obligation will be subject to the following information reporting and backup withholding tax regime. First, payments on the obligation by the issuer or its paying agents will be exempt from information reporting and backup withholding tax unless the issuer or agent has actual knowledge that the payee is a US person. Second, payments on the obligation by a non-US office of a custodian, nominee or other agent of the beneficial owner that has any of certain substantial connections with the US (a 'US-related custodian') will be exempt from information reporting and backup withholding tax if the custodian has documentary evidence in its files that the payee is not a US person (and does not have actual knowledge that the evidence is false) and certain other conditions are met. Third, payments on the obligation by a non-US office of any custodian, nominee or other agent of the beneficial owner that is not a US-related custodian will be exempt from information reporting and backup withholding tax.

C. US ISSUERS AND NON-US ISSUERS WITH SUBSTANTIAL US CONNECTIONS: NON-EXEMPT OBLIGATIONS

An obligation of a US issuer (or of a non-US issuer with a substantial US connection) that does not satisfy the applicable requirements described above

---

28 This legend differs from the legend that an obligation is required to bear in order to comply with the TEFRA Eurobond exception.

will not qualify as an exempt obligation. Payments on such a 'non-exempt' obligation generally will be subject to information reporting and backup withholding tax unless the payee (i) is a corporation, or (ii) establishes its exempt non-US status by providing a Form W–8 or Form 1001.

Issuers and their paying agents may not be overly concerned with the non-exempt nature of an obligation because they tend to make payments only to the clearing organisations or to other corporate entities. On the other hand, custodians holding obligations issued pursuant to a non-exempt euronote issuance facility or Euro-commercial paper programme for the account of a non-corporate beneficial owner generally will be required to obtain a Form W–8 or Form 1001 from the beneficial owner in order to avoid the imposition of information reporting and backup withholding tax; the extent to which this requirement will pose a marketing problem for such programmes is not entirely clear.

D. NON-US ISSUERS WITHOUT SUBSTANTIAL US CONNECTIONS

Obligations of a non-US issuer that does not have a substantial US connection are exempt from information reporting and backup withholding tax except to the extent that payments on the obligation are made within the US. For this purpose, and in the absence of actual knowledge to the contrary, a custodian or other middleman may treat a corporate issuer as a non-US corporation if its name reasonably so indicates and may treat such a corporation as an issuer that does not have a substantial US connection. However, a paying agent of, or a middleman having a contractual relationship with, the non-US corporation must receive a statement, signed under penalties of perjury, from the secretary or other authorised representative of the non-US corporation stating in effect that the corporation does not have a substantial US connection. Payments made within the US on an obligation of a non-US issuer are fully subject to information reporting and backup withholding tax.

ENGLISH LAW CONSIDERATIONS

(i) Companies Act 1985

The Companies Act 1985 is of particular importance for all participants in the euronote and Euro-commercial paper market. Notes issued pursuant to a euronote issuance facility or a Euro-commercial paper programme can be classified as what the Act calls 'debentures'. Any written invitation – whether notice, circular or advertisement – offering these notes to the public for subscription or purchase is considered to be a 'prospectus' and requires to be lodged with the Registrar of Companies and to comply with the provisions of the Act. A prospectus is a document of considerable importance providing significant detail about the issuer and the securities being offered and it is required to be issued each time securities are offered to the public. Under English civil law every person who has authorised the issue of the prospectus would be liable to compensate purchasers, in our case, of notes who have suffered loss as a result of inaccurate or misleading information contained in the prospectus. This liability might apply to the lead manager/dealer as well as the issuer.

For the issuer a prospectus involves considerable preparation and disclosure and, insofar as it relates to Euro-commercial paper, a prospectus would, strictly speaking, need to be prepared and issued each time notes are offered. In a regularly or continuously offered programme this is clearly impracticable as it would be even if the notes were listed on the Stock Exchange (an alternative to complying with the provisions of the Act). Issuers and dealers alike have therefore turned their attention to the definition of prospectus to determine whether requirements to issue a full detailed prospectus can be avoided.

Two elements of the Companies Act definition are critical in this regard – what is a 'prospectus, notice, circular, advertisement, or other invitation' and what constitutes 'offering to the public'?

The latter is the easier to clarify. The 'public' means virtually any investor whether a private individual or a professional investor. The definition is intended to capture any investor. However, for an issuer incorporated outside Great Britain – even if it has a place of business in that country – an offering of its euronotes or Euro-commercial paper is not deemed to be made 'to the public' if the notes are offered only to persons whose 'ordinary business' it is to buy or sell shares or debentures, whether as principal or agent. This is termed the 'professionals' exemption' and all foreign issuers of euronotes and Euro-commercial paper use it to have their paper sold. For sovereign issuers the Act does not apply in this regard and they may issue paper and dealers may offer it without hindrance.

However, English companies wishing to issue notes risk having any written material sent to potential investors in conjunction with an oral (ie telephone) or other offer made by a bank or dealer considered a prospectus. Because of this most English companies hitherto have used an overseas subsidiary as the issuing vehicle making use of the 'professionals' exemption' and on-lending the proceeds under a suitable double-tax treaty. British issuers do not therefore enjoy the same flexibility with regard to the professionals' exemption as foreign issuers.

The first element mentioned above, ie what a prospectus actually is, becomes highly relevant at this point. A central issue has been whether the offer is oral or written. If a dealer telephones a potential investor, describes the issuer, quotes a yield and sells a note the consensus view is that this does not constitute a 'prospectus'. It becomes more complicated where a telephone offer is made and written material is despatched to the potential investor who will then read it and, if it finds the information satisfactory, will then purchase a note. Whether this constitutes a prospectus is a moot point. Suffice to say that until the Financial Services Bill is enacted and its provisions clarified, the issue and sale of notes issued by an English company is a potential legal minefield which requires careful analysis by issuers, dealers and their legal advisors.

(ii) Prevention of Fraud (Investments) Act 1958

This Act concerns euronote and Euro-commercial paper market participants in that it imposes (s 13) criminal liability on persons making fraudulent, misleading or dishonest statements or the concealment of material information in connection with a sale of notes.

Section 14, however, permits the distribution within or from Great Britain of circulars or information for the purposes of selling notes by or to professionals involved in the securities markets. This, therefore, would include exempted dealers, licensed dealers, members of recognised associations of dealers in securities and those whose business involves the buying, holding or selling of securities. Euro-commercial paper dealers falling into the first part of the definition are free to distribute material provided they do so to professionals only.

(iii) Banking Act 1979

This Act was passed to regulate the acceptance of deposits in the course of a business and conferred various functions on the Bank of England with respect to the control of institutions carrying on deposit-taking businesses.

The construction of the Act, and in particular section 1, is very wide both as regards what constitutes a deposit and what constitutes carrying on a deposit-taking business. The Bank of England takes the view that even the acceptance of one deposit may constitute carrying on a deposit-taking business. Accordingly in circumstances where the issuer is not itself a recognised bank or licenced institution (licenced under the Banking Act) then it is necessary for the issuer, particularly if it is an English issuer, to have regard to the provisions of the Banking Act. However, it is generally accepted that the provisions of the Act do not apply in the case where the currency in question is not sterling. Therefore Eurodollar notes issued under a Euro-commercial paper programme are deemed to fall outside the Act.

(iv) Withholding tax and stamp duties

As with Eurobonds, it is important for investors in euronotes and Euro-commercial paper to be able to receive any interest payable gross. It will, of course, be important to ensure that this is permissible under the local laws of the issuer and it is not appropriate in this book to discuss the detailed provisions contained in any jurisdiction. Similarly it is important to ensure that no stamp duties are applicable in respect of the agreements being executed or on the issue of notes.

Conversely, from the point of view of the issuer, it is important for it to ensure that under its local tax laws it is able to treat any income paid as deductible expense and, in the case of the United Kingdom, both this and the ability to pay net of withholding tax is possible. With regard to the payment net of withholding tax the preferred route adopted by United Kingdom issuers has been to issue their paper at a discount to yield and such a strategy has found some favour amongst other issuers.

CHAPTER 8

Prospects for the future

The previous chapters have attempted to analyse, evaluate and illustrate the past and present euronote and Euro-commercial paper markets. A number of key trends have been identified as influential factors on issuers, intermediaries and investors alike in bringing about an active and maturing Euro-commercial paper market. The most important of these trends have been:

- fierce competition between banks for borrowers mandates;
- a continuing decline in lending margins;
- preoccupation with and disagreement over distribution techniques; and
- general nervousness about commercial bank creditworthiness.

Now that a Euro-commercial paper market has been established and is thriving a number of these trends seem to be less important with regard to the future of the market. With the decoupling of underwriting from note placement the decline in lending margins has become a less relevant issue. Issuers able to command sub-LIBOR yields on their paper could only be tempted back into bank loans if banks were prepared to match those yields. This would require a recognition by banks that LIBOR is not a cost of funds benchmark. Should that happen, pressure on return on capital would make it difficult for banks to accept sub-LIBOR pricing.

As the debate over distribution techniques has been effectively closed by the general acceptance of the Euro-commercial paper programme as the most efficient and flexible structure, fewer euronote issuance facilities are being arranged. Whilst fierce competition still exists among banks for borrower mandates, these seem increasingly to be for straightforward revolving credits. This is taking Euro-commercial paper out of the competitive environment for committed facilities which was largely responsible for its genesis.

Of those key trends cited above, only the decline in the creditworthiness of the commercial bank sector is as strong a factor as it was two or three years ago. Arguably, with the problems that this sector continues to face, the trend is even more strongly felt today. The risk diversification process will probably continue to act as a spur to the market.

But Euro-commercial paper has developed a momentum of its own. Regarded increasingly as the optimum money market instrument, it can offer:

- a wide and widening range of issuers in the bank, corporate and sovereign sectors;
- excellent liquidity provided by a group of large and skilful dealers;
- settlement procedures which are straightforward and cost-effective;
- a growing number of issuers willing to provide constant (or regular) amounts of paper for a wide range of maturities.

None of these features can be regarded as a source of complacency for participants in the market. In particular, there is a real need for more flexible issuers, those which will give constant availability and a wide range of maturities. Intermittent issuers which merely wish to impose their own maturity requirements on the market can only take the market so far before it becomes too inflexible. As we have observed, the flexible programme is often the most cost-competitive.

Looking forward, participants in the Euro-commercial paper market are faced with a variety of questions and considerations which make it one of the most fascinating areas in the financial marketplace today.

GROWTH

Estimates at the end of 1986 of the size of the Euro-commercial paper market find a consensus around $30 billion. Forecasts for growth of the market must take several factors into consideration, not least the performance of the long-term bond and equity markets. Money market instruments are treated by many as a medium for the investment of temporary liquidity between long-term investment decisions and strengthening bond and equity markets could divert funds away from the Euro-commercial paper market. Investors' view of the US-dollar will also be important – if a weakening is expected then fewer investors will have US dollars to invest. The risk diversification process should however continue to push funds out of time-deposits, FRNs and CDs into the Euro-commercial market. Growth forecasts can therefore only be subjective and couched with caveats, though a number of market participants expect a $50 billion market by the end of 1987.

CURRENCY COMMERCIAL PAPER

Certain European countries – the Netherlands, France and the UK – have established a local currency commercial paper market. Other countries might follow suit and this would provide a parallel set of local currency commercial paper markets to the Euro-commercial paper market. Investors holding local currency would therefore have an investment option additional to their current range. As we have seen, dealers operating through the foreign exchange markets presently sell Euro-commercial paper to those currency investors on a hedged basis and the emergence of local markets might 'cannibalise' Euro-commercial paper sales made in this way. At the very least it would make the pattern of Euro-commercial paper sales more subject to movements in foreign exchange markets. This will be a very interesting and important area to watch develop.

'COMPOSITE' INDEX

In the domestic commercial paper market participants use the 'Federal Composite' as an index of yields against which rate performance can be measured. Based on actual issuing yields this is an appropriate and consistent index compiled by the Federal Reserve. No such index exists yet in the Euro-commercial paper market though there are moves to establish one. The benefit would lie in initiating a move away from the imperfect LIBID/LIBOR benchmark and into an index generated by purely Euro-commercial paper yields to which all issuers could compare their own issuing yield. The aim would be to select a group of regular issuers of the highest quality creditworthiness and for dealers to input actual issuing yields to a third party which would administer the compilation and publication of the index.

EUROPEAN RATING AGENCY

We have discussed the unfamiliarity of non-US issuers with the rating process and the prejudice against a US-style analysis of a non-US business enterprise. Some feel the answer to this problem lies in the foundation of a European rating agency which would be staffed by professionals familiar with the accounting conventions and business practices of European (or non-US) companies. Clearly a European rating agency would have to be a non-bank institution and its task to compete with large, professional and widely recognised US rating agencies cannot be underestimated.

EURONOTES VERSUS EURO-COMMERCIAL PAPER

With fewer euronote issuance facilities being arranged it is probable that euronotes as a percentage of the total market will decline. However, active tender panels under long-term committed facilities, provided they are successful, will probably not be changed other than to allow direct bidding. Consequently a substantial amount (though a declining percentage) of euronotes will remain in the market for the foreseeable future. Whether notes issued through the direct bidding method in a euronote issuance facility constitute euronotes or Euro-commercial paper is a moot point but, provided that the direct bidding method is flexible enough to cater for most investors' needs, the distinction may be irrelevant.

NUMBER OF DEALERS

The domestic US commercial paper market is dominated by about six or seven investment banks and, given the size of the Euro-commercial paper market, it is a logical assumption that the situation could be replicated in Europe. A determining factor will be profitability and since this depends to a large extent on sales volume the Euro-commercial paper market, viewed on a purely economic basis, will probably not be able to sustain more than six to eight large dealers.

BANK PROGRAMMES

As banks tend to be constant and volume issuers the proportion of bank paper in the market may begin to outweigh the volume of corporate and sovereign paper. The Euro-commercial paper market might well become a predominantly bank-paper market.

The above are only a small number of issues facing participants in the Euro-commercial paper market and there will be no shortage of competition, innovation and energy from participants responding to those issues. With a market size estimated at about $30 billion at the end of 1987, most participants expect continuing growth thereby consolidating the position of Euro-commercial paper as one of the most dominant and flexible money market instruments, offering the widest range of yields and credit risk.

Index